Storytelling 2 Success

The Hero Maker Blueprint
to connect faster and more deeply
with your clients and prospects

DOUG KLIEWER

Copyright © 2014 Douglas A Kliewer

All rights reserved.

ISBN-10: 1500985112
ISBN-13: 978-1500985110

DEDICATION

Dedicated to my incredible children Corrin, Bryce, and Trey. You are my inspiration to be the best storyteller. Your constant support gives me the foundation to stand upon and proclaim to the world. Words cannot describe how much I love each of you.

TABLE OF CONTENTS

Acknowledgments

Introduction

1	**Why?**	1
2	**Why the Attraction to Story**	9
3	**Crafting a Story**	12
4	**Why You need to Start with Story**	26
5	**The Hero Maker Blueprint**	56
6	**Celebrate Transformational Success of Hero's**	80
7	**Tell a Client Hero Story**	88
8	**Where to Use the Story**	98
9	**All Over the Place Storytelling**	106
10	**Marketing Problem equals Storytelling Problem**	116
11	**Sell with Story**	122
12	**Customer Service Story**	129
13	**Final Story, until…**	134

About the Author

Resources

ACKNOWLEDGMENTS

To try and list the hundreds of people who have been influential in this book is a daunting task and unachievable. There are a few that come to mind in no particular order of importance.

A huge thank you to my dear friends Tom and Marie O'Hara who believed in me from the very beginning about a book project.

Many thanks to Jim and Ellie Folkers for your initial trust in me as an advisor and then the growth into a wonderful friendship.

To Tom and Jennifer Stearns, your friendship is something that I hold as special. You inspire me with your love for life amidst a challenging time. You both and Brenna are heroes.

To my all of my Toastmaster friends, thanks for a safe place to practice and learn and grow. Thanks Sheryl for allowing me to share your story.

Thanks to Chelsea Avery and Ryan too. Though it has only been short time, your assistance in shaping my words to speak have been eye opening.

To my boys who challenge and keep me on my storytelling toes, by giving me some interesting characters to pull together in the bedtime stories we create together. Your attentiveness has taught me so much of the power of the story. Your laughter at character voices and continued pleading for more is special each and every time.

Thanks to my beautiful daughter and her chuckles from the other room, and my parents listening through the vents who taught me that we are never too old for a story.

DOUG KLIEWER

To my brother Greg who has always been one of my biggest supporters. This project would not have been to this level, if not for you taking on the arduous task of bringing more clarity to the words I am trying to express. Much love to you, bro!

To my parents for coming along side at a time when I needed you the most. You teach me every day the importance of connection.

To the many authors, product creators, motivational speakers, preachers who have shared a story with the world and therefore teaching me to be more

My 2 Success Master mind group for being there and allowing me a space to bounce ideas off, hold me to the fire and push me to being the best.

I need to thank Mike Koenigs. I have bought his products and been to his conferences and continually see how he promotes his clients, which started my thinking about the Hero Maker Blueprint.

Thank you to my friends who have been there in my hours of need. You have shown what it means to be a friend and I wish many blessing on you. I know that I have missed others of you and apologize in advance. Though not mentioned specifically, you are an essential part of the story that we in. I can't wait to experience story again with you soon.

INTRODUCTION

A book about storytelling for business? At first it didn't make sense. Storytelling is for children's books and movies. How could a business owner or professional take these concepts and use them in the business world?

Then I realized that while storytelling is mostly thought of as the aforementioned communications, it embodies a set of tried and true principles essential to nurture and sustain any business relationship. In fact, these principles will increase our effectiveness to build a lasting business only as we become great storytellers. Soon, traditional advertising will fade away, and what happened for centuries will once again be the tried and true means of relating our businesses to the consumer.

This book has the best of both worlds

There is an art to storytelling and yet it is a science. Let's think of the study of music for a moment, which includes the discipline of time and structure for connecting notes and sounds. This science of music is necessary, otherwise you get a bunch of ear piercing noise. A musician brings artistic flair to this science and inspires us with how they combine these notes and time to draw out emotional connection.

Storytelling will do the same. There will be certain ingredients that are necessary to crafting a story. But you bring this science together in a way that is influenced by your talents to deliver the art of storytelling.

There is work involved in storytelling. But we already tell stories in social settings, and by studying its details you will be able to apply this same craft to your business. I have included some examples, not all of which are business stories because I want you to take the time to examine the processes. There will be truths in each of these stories which naturally apply to the business world.

The art of storytelling needs to be experienced.

What you will find inside are the stable principles. In other words, they work when you implement them. Based on the rock solid strategies I have been using with my clients for years, the results speak for themselves.

Of course, there are elements which change from time to time, and when I or my team came across one of those, we decided to add an online section of this book for those of you who want the latest and greatest. Look for the "Resource" page at the end of the book. That will take you to a page on our website where we host the most current data on a particular topic.

One important piece of advice: use the resources. They will help you get more clients and *more freedom*.

On that note, the difference between average businesses or practices and *great* businesses and practices comes down to implementation. One often differs from another only in their willingness to implement the things they learn.

The same is true for the information in this book. It works, yet similar to everything you learned in school, it only works when implemented. You *knowing* all of this information won't help you make any more money or sell your services or even your practice for more. When you *implement* it, this information, you will help more people, create a more stable business, and maybe even gain some bragging rights at the next conference. Because that is what business is all about, helping more people, and you can do it better and faster by the use of story.

The design and the flow of the book is to give some real life examples of stories I have experienced and use them to reveal some of the hidden gems you can use to tell a better story. By connecting the ordinary to your message through a story, you can and will do some extraordinary things in your business.

Go ahead and use this stuff…and send us your success story. We want to know and hear about them.

A Story is about giving…

At its core the stories that we share with our clients and potential customers is about giving. We give away information. We give a glimpse into our story. We give something of ourselves.

One of the most important types of stories is what I will call a "giving" story. At the core it is using our story to improve another story needing some help. We will learn more later, but more than learning is doing. And to show you the importance of giving away a story, I will be giving away a portion of the purchase price of this book as we join together to help make others story better.

You can learn more when you get to the Resources page. But briefly, there are two stories I wish to help with the publication of this book, 20 Liters and Rett syndrome research.

20 Liters is a project to help the 800 million people around the world who don't have access to clean drinking water. Do you realize that more people die from water related diseases than from all crimes combined? Both stories need to change but we can do something about access to clean drinking water today. How the story around this book will help is that for every 100 books sold, a family of 6 will be supplied with clean drinking water for 10 years.

Rettsyndrome.org is leading the race to find effective treatments and a cure for Rett. Rett is a neurological disease that affects primarily girls. Affecting nearly every aspect of the child's life: their ability to speak, walk, eat, and even breathe easily. The hallmark of Rett syndrome is near constant repetitive hand movements while awake. One dollar from each book sale will be donated to help change this story.

Let's get started

On that note, one of the most common questions I get from business owners is, "How am I supposed to get all of this done?"

The answer is that smart business owners know how to build (or find) good teams. On that note, toward the end of the book we have included a section on where and how to find competent people to help implement your storytelling strategy.

So, let's get started.

CHAPTER 1

WHY?

"He who has a why to live can bear almost any how."

---Friedrich Nietzsche

Congratulations! Just by getting to this first chapter, you're already miles ahead of your competition.

Why?

Well, most people don't take the necessary action for success. You've gotten this far. Now let's go the rest of the way together. At least you're forward thinking; you know the buzzword right now is Story Telling. It is a big deal, or so you have heard. You know that your business is humming along very well. You might be using the internet or online marketing to drum up a little business here and there if you can, and maybe this book on Storytelling can help you maximize your marketing and sales efforts.

DOUG KLIEWER

What's my why?

As a parent of three children, two of them currently in middle school, my kids and I have recently experienced the ups and downs of the middle school life. My son, who is currently in 7th grade, has made me acutely aware of being sometimes "satisfied." If you are a parent, you understand how each one of us wants the best for our kids. But sometimes that is not what we see from our children. As I would feel my frustration boil up with him, I luckily stopped long enough to ask where this frustration was coming from and didn't have to look too far.

It was from me.

I opened my eyes to my own "satisfaction" with where I am in life. I would hear myself say to him, "I don't want you to wake up one day and realize that you could have had so much more." As the sound of those words made their way from my lips to my own ears, I heard another voice inside my head saying, "those are some pretty good words to live by, why don't you put them into practice?"

Ouch!

If you're like me, you've often found yourself listening to a talk or reading a book where the speaker/author pulls out all proverbial stops before climaxing with their most important set of points—the pause, the elevated volume, the admonishment to earmark and reread—and yet you blow right past the section. In my case, I may have even written something down, congratulated myself for the intention and effort and made a mental note to revisit the discussion when I have more time. Right! Just like taking the cap off of a thirst-quenching bottle of water but then setting it down and not allowing it do what it is designed to do, this particular note would sit lost on my bookshelf collecting dust.

Now if this is the first time you're experiencing such a moment, make a mental note of what we are going to discuss here now. If you relate to what I described, then the both of us need to take this next step.

"Next step" implies movement in a direction. Whether or not one actually takes the next step is ultimately a matter of choice. But what I have learned is that many successful plans of action are initiated without a clear understanding of the specific direction in which the actions will ultimately lead. Yes, it is certainly nice when we do have a sense of direction from the start. But often we do not. In these cases the most important thing is that we put an end to inertia and initiate movement, since then there is at least a chance that things will sort themselves out and that direction will become clearer. So sometimes we just have to get moving; sometimes we have to believe in the story

How will you know if you believe it? When you start putting it into practice. You can't have the former without the latter. To believe something is to practice it – i.e. test it.

It won't be perfect. But as Les Brown says, "you have to start in order to be great."

Here is the most important part of what I will write.

I have, for too long, talked about the importance of communicating your story and of realizing the value of your story. We did not come into this world to just be "satisfied". There is so much more to living life. But for far too many of us, we don't think that our story is significant. So we muddle through life trying to force the significance of what we do and how we do it. We describe ourselves in terms of what we think we are. I am a (fill in your occupation/job title).

We hope that people will like us when they find out just how significant is the "what" that we do. Or we point to our training as a way to substantiate our importance and value.

Then I had a meeting with a splendid friend of mine, you know, the one who can break through the fluff you are trying to put out. In one fell swoop they became a hero.

"So Doug, Why?"

One simple word.

A salvation of sorts.

At that moment I listened to my heart. My story was important; that was my "why." A story is a part of our being. If I were to believe that my story was important, then other stories must be important as well. Each of these stories have something to teach us. Each provides way to connect ourselves to each other and the journey we traverse.

I do not mean to imply that I didn't have some notion of significance before. Yes, I admit that my parents and/or societal beliefs have told me such. But believing something verses' putting it into action on a consistent basis is where the shift happens. As stated earlier, action will clarify a belief for someone; you will put into action what you believe.

The journey to teach and encourage others about the importance of our stories began. It was no longer about the widget or excruciatingly detailed descriptions of the widget. Widgets are just widgets, after all. And they always will be. I wanted to know more; I was interested in something else.

I started to ask questions like: tell me why you are a florist, chiropractor, attorney, waitress, hair stylist, musician, realtor, or banker?

Tell me why you build houses, cook meals, teach kids, build filters for clean drinking water, or protect people?

The "why" of each one of these vocations or careers or lines of work is the story. And it is to this that we need to speak in this book

You may think that stories won't help you all that much. People know you. You're in the Yellow Pages, you have a website, you are on all of the social sites, and you're still getting a healthy amount of business.

Is there a correlation between online marketing and stories? Who wants to listen to stories, especially about your local business?

The majority of your potential clients, that's who.

First, let's look at some interesting facts. Recent research shows that the fulfillment of online searches is done overwhelmingly by local businesses. A 2010 study by BIA/Kelsey and research firm ComStat found that before making a local purchase, a staggering 97% of consumers first research their purchase and local services online. It isn't just with local services either. Major e-retailers are being beaten out by customers who research products online but then choose to buy them at local stores. It seems to suggest that while online research has become commonplace, people ultimately like human interaction; they inform themselves online, but in the end they want that personal connection.

Did you see what your consumers want?

Personal connection.

Human interaction.

The consequence of this is two-fold. First, any business with no (or with substandard) online presence is left out of that research process. People want to fulfill their online searches locally. But if you don't pop up when they're doing their research, you'll simply fly under their radar. You'll lose their business to another company that has some online presence.

Second, and perhaps even more importantly, is what happens if and when someone finds you. It speaks volumes about why storytelling is an essential part of this two-edged sword.

You can have an internet presence. You might be attracting consumers to your site, but what is getting them to stick?

Is it the slick and flashy pictures?

I will argue, NO!

Yes, pictures are important to your website. But are they the real reason that it makes someone stick to your website? Pam Grossman from Getty Images says, "The viewer's eye has become a lot more sophisticated and what it wants is real." The story and pictures that tell it need to be real, not some photo-shopped picture of some irrelevant character added to the story. Is it a list of benefits detailing what your widget will do for them?

Again, imperative items that your clients and potential clients might be looking for should be on your page and easily searchable. Yes, we have a chapter on it later on how to talk about your benefits in a story.

What is it that gets them to stick is the connection that they have to you? Remember the study mentioned earlier about human interaction and personal connection. What one thing wanted by your client encompasses these two qualities?

Story! Story! Story!

It is why you need to be a Storyteller, and a pretty darn good one in order to make it in today's business world.

What it's not

Why have we started to put so much emphasis on storytelling? Is it a fad or just some gimmick that the business world needs to learn in order to deceive their prospects and customers into buying? If you think by learning a technique that you will be able to trick a prospect into buying from you, then close this book right now. What we are going to discuss is way deeper than mere surface parlor tricks.

In order for your story to connect with others, you must first connect with it. It is this connection that will inspire you and push deeper into the wonder of the story. And it is only once you have gone there, that will you be able to tell a great story. Only after connecting with the "why" of your own story will you fathom how to connect your story with your prospect or client.

As Paul Smith in *Lead with a Story* states, it is "returning to the natural process." In fact, he goes on to say that, "for most of history, storytelling was a natural part of leadership."

You see, a real leader of an industry, business, sales, or life will always connect at a deep level with the story—first their story and then, interestingly, their client's story.

All right, let's get story crafting.

CHAPTER 2

WHY THE ATTRACTION TO STORY?

"Trust the story ... the storyteller may dissemble and deceive, the story can't: the story can only ever be itself."

---James Robertson, *And the Land Lay Still.*

Think for a moment about the last great movie you watched. What was it about the movie that made it great? Was it the actors or actresses? Was it the superior cinematography or music? Was it directed by an accomplished director?

A great movie will include all the above, but it starts with a great story which also is relatable to us.

Nancy Duarte says, "Stories that expose your humanness and real-life challenges often have the most power to change others, because the audience can relate to them."

Never before has the consumer been able to pick out a fake. Malcolm Gladwell in "Blink" shows us our incredible ability to detect a counterfeit. He describes four or five different situations where the viewer cannot put a conscious finger on what they are seeing but their "gut" tells them to be leery. As time goes by the viewer is able to determine that their "gut" feeling was accurate, and the item or action was determined to be phony.

There is an enormous amount of information bombarding consumers today. They are dazed and confused. More than ever, therefore, it is essential to survival that your business has a good story which elevates it above all the white noise.

At Nike, all senior managers are designated "corporate storytellers." 3M banned bullet points years ago and replaced them with the process of writing "strategic narratives." Procter & Gamble hired Hollywood directors to teach its executives storytelling techniques. Some forward-thinking business schools have even added storytelling courses to their management curriculum. The reason for this is simple: stories can engage an audience in ways logic and bullet points alone never could. "Whether you are trying to communicate a vision, sell an idea, or inspire a commitment, storytelling is a powerful business tool that can mean the difference between mediocre results and phenomenal success" - Paul Smith, *Lead with a Story*

We as humans are built to connect and relate with stories. Today we slide open our iPhone and don't even think about how it first connects to WiFi and then relays digital information to us in a way we can understand. Connect and relay/relate are the very same terms which resonate in a story.

Engineers at firms such as Apple or Google have formulas they follow for achieving these results. Similarly, because our brains remember and relate best around a story, there is a method used to formulate every great story which you can use today. The key is to see it and then use it. Let's go learn how.

CHAPTER 3

CRAFTING A STORY

> "The drawing and the crafting of the story are fun, but it's the overall meaning that matters to me."
>
> ---Brian Michael Bendis

I have participated in Toastmasters for three years now. During that time, I have competed numerous times in different speech contests. I have won a few and, to my greater development, I have lost many more than I have won. Each loss caused me to stop and rethink how I presented and the message I was seeking to provide.

One of the most important things that I have learned during the process of competing is to watch the audience reaction during my speech and then, after the speech, to note how they related to my message, especially when I wove the message into a story. Accomplished speakers are the ones who have mastered the skill of embedding their message inside a story.

There is some work that must go into this story creation. The work is in first determining what basic point or moral you want your listener to hear. If you take time to refine what you want someone to hear, you will inevitably start to see results. By results, I mean a closer relationship with your audience. That does not always mean an immediate sale. What it does mean is that if you continue to build upon the connection between your prospect's story and your story, you will be top of mind (i.e. top of the list) when they do decide to buy.

Connected to story

I recently have met and started to glean some wonderful nuggets from a gentleman here in Grand Rapids. His story is a great one. He started a company from the ground up and grew it until it became profitable and sustainable. At some point a proposition was made to purchase the business, which he accepted. He then took this opportunity to follow some personal passions as well as engage more with family and charitable interests.

Soon after the sale the new ownership started to experience, "shall we say trouble," as he tells it, so much trouble that the company was at risk and his former employees were in danger of losing their jobs.

What did he do with the prospect of this company closing its doors? Nobody would have batted an eye had he stayed on the outside.

But he was connected to his story.

So despite the potential hurdles, obstacles, and loss, this relationship to a story enabled him to connect to his former employee's stories. The stories of their families and the community as a whole moved him. It was because of this connection that he dove back in to see what he could do to resurrect his old company.

I'm not sure if you have tried to resurrect something lately, but it is not easy task. After many hard and stressful hours and after taking on obligations and debts he had not created, he has lead this company back from the brink of bankruptcy. Today this company employees a large number of people and once again is a stable place of employment.

And today my friend tells a great story, not because he seeks something personal from it, but because it enables those listening to learn something about themselves. He tells the story about the workers and how they are more at ease. He tells the story to give hope, that no matter how dismal the prospects, with hard work and determination you can fix things.

Let's start by looking at what makes up a story.

WHAT MAKES UP A STORY?

I asked a friend of mine the other day, "How did you become a florist?" He paused and stroked the brownish grey beard on his chin for a moment.

"As I think about it, when I was a child, my parents had a huge garden in our back yard. My father grew vegetables in the back part, and my mother raised flowers in the front. During the summers growing up, my siblings and I would go out and pull weeds in the garden. With the sun beating down on us and sweat pouring from our brow, we would make our way down rows of beans and beets or corn and cauliflower."

There was a 4-H fair in the town where he lived. My friend started to take vegetables from the garden to compete at the fair. While pulling weeds, he kept his eye open for the straightest and longest five beans that he could find.

One year, he decided to put together a bouquet of flowers from his mother's garden and placed it into the competition at the fair. He gathered the flower of what he thought was the right portion of blues, purples, reds, yellows, and whites. He arranged them, then took it down to the fair and waited for the judges' opinions.

He won a blue ribbon.

It was this confidence at a young age that showed him that he had an eye for design. It has led him to discover his passion for creating beautiful wedding bouquets for couples embarking on the journey of marriage.

3 Basics of a story

On the simplest level, a story is made up of three essential parts. We will be going into it on a deeper level in the next few sections, but let's set the stage. The first part consists of the characters of the story. It is these characters with whom the audience needs to connect by placing themselves into their shoes.

The second is the problem, or we can call it the antagonist. This is someone or something that arrives in the story and causes some type of discomfort or issue. It could be a sickness or catastrophic storm or an individual who does something to harm a main character.

The third and final part of a story is the hero or protagonist. It is the solution to the problem. It is the part of the story we can't wait to see. It is this anticipation that is the real success of the story. The antagonist or problem is now a part of the story, and we all want it to resolve. In fact, we want it resolved yesterday. The hero brings or finds the type of resolution we all seek.

Important factors to consider

Having a grasp on the three basics above will set your storytelling off on a good foot. And as we journey down this path, there are some other important factors we need to discuss.

The first is to know your audience. The success of your story will be dependent on the connection you have with your audience and how they are connected to you.

How does your audience see and hear your story? They look at it from their point of view. Every step along the way they wonder, "What is in the story that I can use in my own efforts. Since I am taking the time to listen to this story, it needs to be relevant to my circumstances."

If you know your audience, know what they want and need, you will be miles ahead of your competition. It's easy to say you know what they want, but many times this is harder than it would appear to be.

To set yourself apart is to know your audience better than they know themselves. If you take the time and do diligent research on your audience, you will find a "smoking gun." A smoking gun refers to the piece of evidence the legal market uses to guarantee that an opponent cannot win. Chet Holmes in *The Ultimate Sales Machine* puts it this way when talking about business research, "There's always that smoking gun that positions you above everyone else...always." But you will only find it by understanding your audience the best. (I list a couple companies that will help you with this at the end of the book.)

A second item, which goes along with knowing your audience, is to remember that you don't want to make your audience uncomfortable, confused, or embarrassed to know you. It is never ok to tell a story to one member of the audience at the expense of another person.

The third item is to set the plot where your characters will be interacting. You want to give them just enough details, and then allow them to use their imagination to fill in the rest. What does that look like to give just enough details?

I attended a speaker training recently being put on by Ryan Avery. Ryan Avery became the youngest World Champion of Public Speaking when he won the Toastmasters International speech contest in 2012. One suggestion he gave that day was to "drop the prop."

Imagine you come to the part of your story that describes you playing basketball. You have a couple of options. You could begin describing in detail how your basketball bears your initials, has a scratch by the Spaulding logo, is an official NCAA basketball, etc. Or you could just say you grabbed your basketball.

By shrinking your description down to "I grabbed my basketball", you have just allowed your listener to fill in the details of the basketball with their sub-conscious. What basketball do you think your client or prospect will place into the story?

Theirs!

What does your basketball look like?

For me it's scuffed up, it has no grip left because I play on an outside court, and you can barely see the Rawlings emblem.

Do you see what needs to happen with the story that you are sharing? You must allow them to make your story their story. They will do this by taking unstated details of your story and substituting in their own. This is a critical step to understand and implement. When you allow your client or prospect to take ownership of your story, you will set yourself apart from every other competitor. You will create a bond, and it is this bond that you must continue to grow and nurture, so that when your customers have a problem, they come to you to gain resolution.

Let's go look deeper at the basics of this story you are going to craft.

CHARACTERS TO ADD

"If a story is not about the hearer he [or she] will not listen... A great lasting story is about everyone, or it will not last. The strange and foreign is not interesting--only the intensely personal and familiar."

---John Steinbeck, *East of Eden*

"Picture to yourself the most beautiful girl imaginable! She was so beautiful that there would be no point, in view of my meager talent for storytelling, in even trying to put her beauty into words. That would far exceed my capabilities, so I'll refrain from mentioning whether she was a blonde or a brunette or a redhead, or whether her hair was long or short or curly or smooth as silk. I shall also refrain from the usual comparisons where her complexion was concerned, for instance milk, velvet, satin, peaches and cream, honey or ivory, Instead, I shall leave it entirely up to your imagination to fill in this blank with your own ideal of feminine beauty."

---Walter Moers, *The Alchemaster's Apprentice*

Characters are the pieces of your story into which your audience will most readily transform themselves. There is something we see at the simplest level in the characters of a story.

At the opposite of the spectrum, you do need to be careful about the type of characters you bring into a story, since characters can disconnect as well as connect.

You must know your audience. Who is that ideal customer? Because when you center your characters around some avatar, for example, you are basically asking your customers to identify with that avatar. Too many times when I hear business people marketing a story, it goes out to people that have no interest or correlation to the characters. How many times have you watched a commercial and asked, "what were they selling?" The creator of the storyline missed what they thought was the core desire of the audience. When you miss this, you are in danger of bringing in characters that the audience does not bond with at all.

Now this is not to say that you might not want to introduce a character who is opposite your audience in order to cause friction, since creating friction in this way might actually help to promote your (the protagonist's) cause by leading the listener to "join the alliance" against the antagonist.

YOU NEED A GOOD PROBLEM

"That which does not kill us *makes* us *stronger*."

---Friedrich Nietzsche

"Story is a yearning meeting an obstacle."

---Robert Olen Butler

It was a rather chilly morning as I headed out for a run. The sun was just rising in the horizon as the first lights of the day entered. As I started down the road, I could see short bursts of steam plow before me as I settled into a solid aerobic pace. I was going to see how far I could go.

About 1 mile into my run my eyes caught the reflection of a distant object glimmering in the rising sun. As I grew closer and closer, there was a curiosity building. When I arrived and noticed what the object was, I bent over, picked it up, and got myself back into a steady pace. In fact, the same experience repeated itself six times that morning. Each time I stopped and picked up the object and continued on my run.

Those glimmering objects became a hero to me that morning. They gave me a ray of hope that still, to this day, amazes me and keeps me going. It was because of those shiny objects that I am inspired to write these thoughts to you today.

What were those objects? Empty soda cans and a couple of beer cans.

How can empty soda or beer cans be a ray of hope? If they were full perhaps, you may think, but not empty. But you need to understand the full story to appreciate the true content of my experience that morning.

My run began that morning from my small upstairs apartment. I had recently gone through a divorce and was scraping by as I worked to make sure that my kids were provided for as they lived with their mom. When I went for my run, I had a spoon full of peanut butter in a container, a can of beans, one egg.

In Michigan where I live those six empty pop/beer cans meant $.60. Combine that with the 3 dimes and 2 nickels in my car drink holder, and I could buy a loaf of bread. Those cans were heroes for me that day.

What's an antagonist....and how can they be good?

An antagonist is someone who is opposed to, struggles against, or competes with another--an adversary. The antagonist is crucial to any story. Every one of us needs this dilemma, this obstacle in our story. As Edmund Burke puts it, "He that wrestles with us strengthens our nerves and sharpens our skills. Our antagonist is our helper. This amicable conflict with difficulty leads us to an intimate acquaintance with our object and compels us to consider it in all its relations. It will not suffer us to be superficial."

We don't like pain. Whether physical or emotional, we tend to avoid it at any cost. But can we instead take this pain we want to avoid and name it for the obstacle that it is?

Also, what happens if this discomfort comes in the most unexpected place and during a time that should be joyous?

Is there ever a day quite like the day a new baby is born into this world? What is it about that girl or boy being born that stops people to see who they are or what are they like. There is hope and anticipation of what this little one will become. They are innocent. They are helpless. They are precious.

What maybe attracts us to a baby is the realization that this little one has not yet experienced hurt or had their first rejection. Perhaps we wish that somehow that would be reality?

Some dear friends of mine were like all expected parents. As they ushered in their little girl, they were amazed and anticipated what she would grow up to be. The first few months were filled with oohs and aahs as they showed off little Brenna. She continued to grow and be the joy of their life.

But some repeated illnesses began to effect little Brenna, raising questions. These led to further testing in order to determine the cause of her symptoms. After long and arduous visits to doctors and specialists, Brenna was diagnosed with Rett syndrome, a very misunderstood condition affecting about 1 in every 13,000 girls. Sadly an antagonist entered my friends' lives.

YOU MUST HAVE A HERO

"Whoever tells the best story shapes the culture."

---Erwin Raphael McManus

"A hero is someone who has given his or her life to something bigger than oneself."

---Joseph Campbell

"Even if you have a great plot, your speech needs characters that fit squarely into the archetypical roles listeners expect to encounter. Adhering to conventional character types amplifies emotional impact. The audience naturally yearns for the hero to succeed and hates the villain for getting in the hero's way."

-Ryan Avery and Jeremy Donovan from *Speaker, Leader, Champion.*

The main character in every story belongs to the hero. It is this character that the story will move about and around. In a great story we are introduced to them early on, which allows the audience to form this lasting connection.

A hero is not invincible. We are not trying to create a Superman or Wonder Woman character when we are telling stories to our customers. Just like the characters in the story, the hero also needs to be relatable. We will talk further about this idea a little later in the book. What I want us to understand here is the goal of connection. That is what the story is doing for you. The parts of the story, the hero being one of them, must then connect.

Protagonist can get nicked up or hurt in some way, and a good story will do just that. In real life pains are objects of avoidance. In stories they galvanize; pains become the dark tunnel inside which the client is stuck, frozen in fear. To their amazement, however, the hero is there as well. They would never have imagined that there was someone out there who has experienced this same problem.

Isn't that true of us at some level? We for a moment think that our situation is unique to us and that the problem we are facing has never been faced by someone else. As business owners, we know this probably is not true. Yet if we are not careful, we will fall into the trap of believing it. By contrast, the message of the hero to the other characters is that "I have been here before? Would you like to know how I made my way out of this dilemma?"

What is the character's response to the hero?

YEAH!

What does this little nuance mean to the story that you will be telling a potential client or current customer? We will look further later in the book, but here is a quick example.

I was helping a chiropractor client with his marketing needs. As we talked about his business and what he ultimately wanted for it, we dove into his past and found out the "why" of his business. What I discovered was that he had one of those hero moments in a dark tunnel.

One summer day as a teenager he was out swimming with some friends. He got up on a floating dock and jumped off into the water and landed on a sunken log. He broke his back. Luckily for him it didn't paralyze him. It was during his recovery that he gained his lifelong passion. The formative part was an experience he had with a chiropractor, and how it brought him back to health.

Today when he has a new individual come into his office wreathing in pain from a hurt back, he can bend down beside them and share with them that he has been in the same place. Having established a personal connection, he then is able to ask, "Would you like to know how to feel better?"

The hero has a choice about how to handle the problem they face. Will they be overcome, wither and die, or will the problem lead them to new heights from where they can transact change. As Richard Rohr says, "growth only comes through suffering and love."

Take my friends and little Brenna from above. Today Rett syndrome has a worthy hero that is stepping into the gap, because my friends have a passion to grow through the difficulty and not cower to it. They want to teach a story of beauty that lies hidden, yet is so evident if only you have eyes to see it.

CHAPTER 4

WHY YOU NEED TO START WITH STORY?

> "It is my opinion that a story worth reading only in childhood is not worth reading even then."
>
> — C.S. Lewis

Why do we tell stories? Or maybe a better question, what is so important about stories? They are in every fabric of our lives. Turn on the TV or watch a video on the internet, and you see the latest news story. Sit down with family or friends to watch a movie and the story unfolds before your eyes. You listen to what took place at school with your teenage daughter.

What did she tell me?

A story!

We tell stories so that the one listening can share in the experience to some level. It allows us to connect at a deeper level than the presentation of mere fact could ever do. Imagine my disappointment if my daughter just says, "a Test, P.E., lunch, and a new song in band." Do you feel any connection?

But is it relevant to my business?

I can hear some say, but my clients want the facts and a detailed layout of what is going to happen next.

Do they?

I know that I get can easily caught up in my "business" and ultimately forget the needs of my clients or prospects. We are all in need and looking for the connection. As Tony Robbins calls one of the basic human needs, wanting to have certainty and connection gives that to us. We are made for connection. Our clients are social species, just like you and I. And by being human, they seek integration into the society around them, and they do it best by exchange of information within a story.

Please don't interpret me as saying that facts and details are not relevant to the business transaction, because they are. What I want us to understand is that in order to get to the point of the facts and circumstances, we need first to connect to our client or prospect with a story. Otherwise we sell a widget today, but any chance of repeated sales or business exits through the doorway with the customer.

So let us take a second to think about the last time you shared an experience with your family, friend, or business associate. What was happening to you as you shared? Was there a confirmation of what you said by them listening more intently and nodding their head, or by a smile coming across their face as they pictured what was happening?

Thus, the first reason we tell stories is that it vouches to our existence. Our listener imagines how they may have experienced a similar struggle or reality.

Think for a moment how powerful that is in the business world. You have a client that comes into your place of business. You start by relaying a story that has happened within your business. You describe to them how you or a particular client (this is the best kind of story, but more on that later) has engaged with an aspect of your business. You lay the characters out for them to meet. You describe what the problem was. You bring in the hero. This client or prospect now connects on a deeper level and confirms that they have made the correct decision to walk into your place of business.

We tell stories so that we can share experiences in life and bring understanding among ourselves. Humans are social species and telling stories is a mode through which they exchange information. Stories also offer entertainment and integration into society.

On the blogpost, *Why we tell Stories*, the author Vallez describes three reasons for story telling:

http://www.weareovermind.com/why-we-tell-stories/

> *The first reason is for affirmation. In sharing ourselves through our stories, our audiences affirm us as human beings by listening to us. Through their reactions in the twists and turns in our daily adventures, we find someone else relating to us and reminding us that we share common experiences with other people.*
>
> *The same is true for the audiences. They are affirmed as human beings through our stories. They see themselves in*

our stories. They are reminded, through our struggles and pains in the stories that we tell, of their struggles.

And so story telling is in a way a sort of communion, a building of a community through the exchange of inner lives. Humanity affirms itself in storytelling. In storytelling, we are reminded that we are not alone.

The second reason is for healing. It is interesting to note that most storytelling, even in the olden times, occurs at the dinner table. We enjoy eating while exchanging stories. Meals are boring without stories. A family that never talks at the dinner table is most likely a dysfunctional one.

Even in prehistoric times, cavemen share stories of the hunt around the fire while they have their meal. This relationship between storytelling and eating has a very significant meaning for us. While we nourish our bodies when we eat, we nourish our souls when we exchange stories.

Stories heal us when we imagine the heroes who are wounded in their actions while the story unfolds before us. It's not so much that we take pleasure in their misfortunes, but we heal because of their triumph. Even if the stories we listen to are tragedies, even if the protagonists do not win in the end, it is enough to realize that their struggles were worth it—that man is worth redeeming.

Through stories, we understand our woundedness in the universality of the narrative, and we also come to realize that we too, though wounded, are worthy of redemption. Through human struggles in stories, also known as conflict, we begin to heal our very own wounds with hope. If these heroes can struggle, triumph, and are worthy of redemption, so are we. We find something akin from their inner lives to ours.

Through stories, we commune with the characters.

There is a third form of communion in story telling that is explained by the third reason we tell stories. The third reason men tell stories are primarily to address man's greatest fear—an unknown, which is death. Men tell stories to be immortal.

In the transmission of stories to our family members and audiences, we immortalize ourselves as storytellers. Knowing that we are temporal and that we will not live forever, we know that our stories can continue to the last generation of men. We become immortal in our stories.

But this immortality should not be looked at as a vain attempt to extend one's life and fame. Man discovered immortality through story telling so he can commune with generations to come. This is our attempt to be in communion with the future.

Storytelling is Communion

Having grown up in a church environment, I am familiar with the frequent discussions of meaning surrounding the practice of communion. But the more I thought about Vallez's statement about "communion in storytelling," the more I have become convinced that story and storytelling are communion.

After repeatedly doing something for a long time, it is easy to lose sight of its value. The same was true of communion for me, until I went to a deeper level of practice. I started to place myself in the story as if I was an integral part of it.

If a character had to endure through a difficult time, I imagined going through it and also physically tried to experience it.

Here is what I mean. Many religions include the ritual of fasting, abstaining from all food. You can imagine what it might be like to fast. But it is another thing actually to go without food for a period of time. What do you do when the growl in your stomach is as loud as a lion standing next to your ear?

Communion to me is connection with someone or something on a level where you are unable to determine the distinction between these two separate entities. One definition may be the: *interchange or sharing of thoughts or emotions; intimate communication.*

Why is this important to us in business?

We are unable to connect to the problem that a client or prospect is experiencing until we first go through that same issue. Storytelling is displaying to your customers that you have been where they have been. We know the feeling of not eating. We know how it affects us physically and the emotions it creates. (I'd follow this up with a couple of trivial business examples: we know the feeling of a sore back, delayed shipments, timelines in jeopardy, etc.)

I remember too well how people act when they are hungry. I spent eight years in the restaurant industry, where I had many firsthand experiences of patron reactions to order mess ups in the kitchen. The other members of the party would already have their food and be happily eating. Then there would be this one individual who would have to sit and wait patiently while everyone else satisfied their natural cravings—or wait impatiently, as the case may be!

I remember one specific patron who went on a minute long, anger filled tirade to the cashier. This cashier cowered as the person took all their frustration out on them. I was in the kitchen at the time and quickly rushed to the scene of the outburst. After rescuing the cashier from the rant, I spent the next 5 minutes diffusing the situation, apologizing to the customer and relating similar experiences from my own past as an unhappy customer. By the time they left we were laughing together, and they always made sure to say "hi" whenever they returned.

If you have been on either side of this situation, then you already relate to what I am describing. You being able to diffuse a strenuous situation is understanding everything that is happening. And by taking that time, you more than likely have a story to relate to it.

A story will and does bring you to that place of connection each one of us is seeking. The best businesses are those which have experienced the problem they are trying to solve. Start with the story. Live in the story and see how your business will get better.

THE PSYCHOLOGY OF STORY CONNECTS

"Stories give color to black and white information."

---Todd Stocker, *Refined: Turning Pain Into Purpose*

You remember the saying, "a picture paints a thousand words" Why is that? But maybe the more important question is; "Who should paint the picture?"

Ty Bennett, author of *The Power of Storytelling*, further drills down wonderfully when he states, "Its the audiences emotional reaction that creates connection, causes engagement, stimulates learning, solidifies memory, and causes them to take action."

Here is the most important item that I have learned and teach to the speakers that I train. You must connect with you audience in order to get your message across. It does you no good if you have a perfect word for word speech or presentation. If the message that you are trying to convey is not connecting with the audience, you will not be heard. I can't say it more clearly.

We must remember the science around communication broached in earlier chapters. It is worth repeating here again. Communication is 8% words. The other 92% is body language and tonality. 92%! Where does the connection happen? It happens in the sub-conscious of your listener. Their sub-conscious mind is constantly working to form a connection to the message it is hearing. If we can express a message that is inviting and safe through body language and tone, then our sub-conscious mind will start to relive our stories that are similar in nature. It will replace the story it hears with a story that is has lived.

At its most basic level, perhaps, your sub-conscious mind is asking questions around fight or flight. What kind of action do I need to take in order to continue existence? There is a tension that lies in between these type actions. I believe when we tell stories that our sub-conscious mind goes into a "stay" mode. It sits in the middle of this tension and is at peace with not having to struggle over this tension.

When out prospecting to sell someone on the value or benefit of a widget or service, we invoke this fight or flight response in them. When our actions or words cause someone to flee or fight, we have not understood the problem in which the prospect is living.

I know that I have done this many times in the past, where I then try to pigeon hole them into a product or service. Do we fight them back by trying to "fix" them, whatever the cost? Is that really fixing them? Or do we descend to the other end of the spectrum where our own flight mechanics causes us to avoid the real problem as if it never existed?

What kind of world do we create when we ourselves choose to fight or flight? We have created a smaller world of fear and lost out on a bigger world that becomes possible when we connect with our prospect.

What storytelling is going to allow us to do is stay in a place that is open, big and spacious. Choose connection over fear by having a confidence in your own story. It will generate an environment where our whole mind will be able to function and be more creative.

The Emotion to Connect

Jeff Goins eloquently gives us three different keys to engaging the emotion of our clients and prospects in his article *Tell Story*. http://goinswriter.com/tell-story/

He says -

>   *1. Use a hook*

A "hook" is your opener. It's the attention-getter, the question or quote that immediately hooks your listener or reader. The more off-the-wall or mysterious, the better.

Dare your audience to get lost in the story.

2. Tell the story

A story has natural momentum to it. If you simply state what happened in chronological order (many people neglect doing this), you will captivate your audience.

Ira Glass calls this the "anecdote" — a story in its purest form — and likens it to a train on which you've invited others to join. Those riding along can feel that you're heading towards a destination.

Glass also says you need "bait" to keep your audience engaged. As he defines it, bait is a series of implicit or explicit questions you, the storyteller, raise.

Just remember: any question you raise, you'll need to answer. Otherwise, you'll leave the listener in perpetual suspense.

3. Reflect

Many people seem to tell stories just to tell them. But when you start asking why people share (and listen to) stories, often there is an objective. A reason. It may be to encourage or inspire or cause you to think differently. But still there is a purpose to the telling.

At the end of your story, take a moment to reflect on what you shared. Answer any questions you've raised:

- *Why is this relevant?*
- *What's the moral or point?*
- *Who is this message for?*

Help us, the audience, understand what we're supposed to get from the story. It doesn't have to be cliche or cheesy; in fact, your reflection can even be subtle. Just make it count.

In order for a story to effect some change, we must engage on an emotional level that is outside the details of our business. We must go beyond the details and enter into a space that may be unknown but is just as real as the widget we are selling.

The Problem in a Story

This statement seems paradoxical. The problem is necessarily unwanted, but essentially needed. (I now better see what you were after with your original claim that stories are paradoxes. I think this does a better job of expressing your point. Stories are not paradoxes but the problems which drive them are paradoxical in the sense that we don't want them there though they must be there for the story to operate. So while this technically is still not a paradox since paradoxes appeal to cognitive processing as opposed to wants—paradoxes are puzzles of sorts which have no obvious conscious or unconscious solutions—your discussion now makes more sense to someone like myself who understands what these terms mean.

In reality, the problem in a story is taking the characters beyond our initial understanding or intelligence. There is a tension that is created with the problem. The problem will take us into those spaces that our rational or conscious mind cannot enter, unless it has first been opened by our subconscious mind. Stories at the deepest level then allow us to connect to the memories and imaginations of our past, which are stored in our subconscious brain. How is this possible? Can there be a benefit to us ascending to this level? These are great questions to contemplate and let's work through answering them now.

I once heard Paul E. Scheele describe the power of our subconscious mind. He explained it something like this, "imagine you are holding a flashlight and shining it down on your feet. That circumference from the flashlight beam describes your conscious or rational brain. Now from the edges of that circle around your feet, go out eleven miles in each direction, and that gives you a picture of how large your subconscious is in comparison."

The story is going to allow you to connect into this vast storage unit of images and memories. It is where the connection starts to form. And it is all around the story. Our mind is an amazing thing. If we can tap into it and tap into the full experiences of our customers and prospects, we will be able to bring about change.

Storytelling is like good writing. The key to both is to first to pick up on all the subtleties implicit both in your ideas and in the language you are using to express those ideas, and second to manage/organize all that in a way that flows seamlessly and yet leaves nothing untouched—i.e. is complete. It truly is an art form, which partly means that there is no single perfect way to pull it all off. It also means that readers may not pick up on everything, at least not consciously. But at least it is all there to be picked up on, as it were. Both draw upon a certain subconscious digestion process on behalf of the reader/listener.

Story is the key. In fact, there is one type of story that is the key that unlocks it all, but we first need to describe several more essential components of a story. Understanding these aspects of a story will allow you the ability to create and deliver the true message of your business. Once your message is received, then sales and repeat sales can happen. But let's not jump ahead too far. We need to get back to comprehending a story.

MAKE STORY MEMORABLE AND INTERESTING

"The stories we tell literally make the world. If you want to change the world, you need to change your story. This truth applies both to individuals and institutions."

--Michael Margolis

To give a story with the most impact is to commit to only bringing a message. What is it that your product does that changes the lives of those who touch it? If you and your company can attach themselves to a story around a message of changed lives, do you think they will be able to connect with a client? No matter who is servicing or selling them?

As we discussed communion at the end of the last chapter, connecting yourself to the story will give you a firsthand connection to the story. Storytelling to grab someone's attention makes you descriptive and imaginative. In order to best describe and bring to the imagination a scene, you must have lived through it.

To help illustrate, here is a section from a speech that I gave at a state level competition:

As I extended my hand to my daughter, my mind raced back to the future, in a Michael J Fox Deloran time machine to

March, 2000. I was in my chair in awe of the little present nestled on my chest. Her knees tucked up under, her little bottom...pointed in the air. The scent of baby shampoo gently lifted from her full head of hair. A sight that would make any balding man jealous.

My father was there in his coke bottle glasses and suspenders to impart his wisdom

"Son she looks innocent now, but there's this thing called teenager. Remember, Love never gives up...and whoa that's a lotta hair"

Being a new dad was great. The next three years were spent reading bedtime stories, coloring princesses and changing stinky diapers

There was one day when my wife's panicked voice pierced through our home.

"I can't find Corrin! She was in the sandbox. And now she's gone."

We frantically looked in every nook and cranny.

Hopes of we'll find her, soon faded to worry, and then collapsed into sheer...terror

The woods?

Out the door, I flew…like Carl Lewis

As I rounded the bend, I saw…pig tails bobbing up and down running toward me, ecstatic to show me the stash she had found.

I scooped her up; she squealed.

I kissed her raspberry stained cheeks.

She placed one of her prized possessions in my mouth. My taste buds erupted with fresh out of the oven, raspberry pie, ala mode and a prickly stem.

Later that night talking with my father, he said, "You learned in your searching, that Love never gives up…and you did save me a piece of the pie?"

For each of these scenes that I told the audience that night, I took myself back to the actual memory. It became more than descriptive words for me. I remembered that night when I and my newborn daughter fell asleep together on the chair. I could still smell the freshly washed hair. I saw the lime green onesie she wore. I tasted the fresh, slightly squeezed, prickly black raspberry that was placed in my mouth. I heard the squeal when she first caught a glimpse of me. The memory is still fresh even though it has been over a decade since it happened.

If you want to tell a memorable story, then your story must be a part of your mind. When it happens, your audience, in this case your customers, can now take this memory of yours and start to replace it with their memory of a similar story. It is at this moment of replacement that the connection happens, just like putting a plug in the socket. The electricity is available instantaneously, as is the customer contact.

Learning from Memory

Dominic O'Brien, who is the 8x World Memory Champion, says that association is the first key in making things memorable. He uses a short story around this association to help in his memorization techniques. In his article titled, *Every Child Can Win the Memory Game,* O'Brien teaches five strategies that teachers can use to help their students remember. The first method he mentions is the story method; "*To remember a set of information, create a story that links all the elements together. In chemistry, for example, the noble gases are helium, neon, argon, krypton, xenon and radon. Imagine taking off in a helium balloon lit up with a neon light. An argon welder turns into Superman, who takes you to the planet Krypton, and so on.*"

If our business is growing and continues to be a strong, it must be remembered. Story as O'Brien says, will help us keep that memory going in the lives of our clients.

By telling a story with a message, you will set yourself apart from all your competition. When telling your story make sure that it is relatable and compelling. If you include these couple elements in your story, you will create a story capable of attracting and retaining prospects and you will build relationships sufficiently strong to turn clients into raving fans.

DOUG KLIEWER

Laugh a little

Humor is another important feature to help engage your listener. When we smile and laugh, we release the chemical, endorphin, into our bodily system. This chemical places us in a state to start to build likeability and relationship.

I earned the opportunity to compete in a humorous speech contest at the district level for Toastmasters. My speech was titled, "Admitting you have a problem is the first step to recovery." It was my fun look at how I had progressed from reading stories to my children to now making them up. My two boys are emphatic that I make up a story for them, even though they are at the age that bedtime stories are for "little kids." During the speech, I throw in some impersonations and funny perspectives from our interactions. What was interesting is that over the next two days after the speech, people I didn't know from the conference would open conversation up with me, "I loved your cow impersonation or this piece of the story made me laugh." Six months later I meet someone, whose first comment was, "Your the gentleman who did the cow impersonation." Not that you want to be known as a "cow" impersonator, but humor was the connector that made it memorable. It can also be for you. Find that story that you can bring laughter into the discussion.

Seven *powerful steps for interesting stories!*

I saw these steps on a blog post from Hansen Communication Lab characterize how we tell an interesting story.

STORYTELLING 2 SUCCESS

Throughout time, the greatest orators and teachers have illuminated their lessons by telling powerful stories. Storytelling is a great way to engage your audience and show them how your topic, point or lesson relates to them specifically. Unfortunately, not everyone is born a great story-teller, and some stories are better than others. Follow these 7 steps to delivering great stories every time!

1. Know your audience and make sure your story is appropriate.

When telling stories it is really important to know who you are telling them to and have an idea of how they might react to them. Age group, professional level and culture are extremely important factors; make sure your story is appropriate for your audience. Even when you are telling a "tried and true" story, what might be appropriate and funny for one group, could be distasteful and unacceptable for another. Take care when choosing the topic of your story and the language you use to deliver it.

2. Make your story easy to relate to.

The topics of stories should be broad enough that anyone can relate to them. Comedians use this tactic in their stand-up comedy. The funniest comedians take every-day situations that everyone experiences and make light of them. It is what a good story does. It has a plot that everyone can relate to, a subject that is simple, straightforward and illustrative of the lesson. If you've chosen the right story and delivered it correctly, you will see the light bulbs going off above people's heads. If you have to say, "I guess you had to be there," you have not told a clear and effective story!

3. Write out your story... and cut it in half.
I have seen way too many speakers go on and on about things where I just want to stand up and yell, "Can you make this long story short?" When you plan to tell a story for the first time, write it out the way you want to present it... and then cut it in half. Remember the KISS philosophy: Keep it Short and Simple. Give us the nuts and bolts and nothing else. Sometimes story-tellers get wrapped up in the details, usually because they experienced the situation and found those details relevant. But usually the details of what you were wearing at the time and where you bought that outfit are not adding to the lesson or plot of the story.

4. Have a clear link between your story and your lesson.
A story is only worth telling if it has an obvious link to the subject being taught. We all know from common conversation how annoying it is to listen to someone's long-winded story just to wonder at the end of it why it was shared. Effective speakers have a very clear link between the moral of their stories and the topic at hand. If this link is missing, the story is useless, and your listeners are left wondering what it was.

5. Engage your listener by engaging their senses.
A good story-teller engages all of our senses. We might listen to you tell a funny story about ice cream, and that will be enjoyable, but what if you could make us taste that ice cream, feel its creamy consistency on our tongues, visualize the mess that's made all over your face as a child, and so on. That's what will make your story great and memorable.

6. Be aware of audience cues when telling your story.
As a speaker, you should always be aware of audience response. The attentive speaker will always know when the audience is losing interest and make appropriate changes to the delivery of the story, the language being used, the topic or even the final moral or punch-line. Different audiences won't always react to the same story the same way. No matter how well you do your homework, you can still run into problems. Be flexible and have a back-up plan if your story isn't going as well as planned.

7. Deliver your story with some feeling!
The key to an amazing story is in its delivery. A passionate storyteller will get much more enthusiastic response from the listeners than a boring one! Use variations in pitch, volume and intonation to make the story interesting to listen to. Be sure to pause at the right times for dramatic effect, and pull the audience in with mystique and excitement.
http://www.hansencommlab.com/storytellingbasics.html

We have the inner workings to making a story that is memorable and interesting. Each will be essential as we work toward implementing the Hero Maker Blueprint. There is a couple of aspects that we need to discuss first. Let's talk a bit about making our story relatable.

RELATION TO STORY

"The human species thinks in metaphors and learns through stories."

--Mary Catherine Bateson

"It is a law of the story-teller's art that he does not tell a story. It is the listener who tells it. The story-teller does but provides him with the stimuli."

---Melville Davisson Post, *Uncle Abner The Doomdorf Mystery*

My speaking coach continues to remind me of the importance of knowing my audience. How are you going to relate your message to them? The definition of relatable found on dictionary.com is: to bring into or establish association, connection or to establish a social or sympathetic relationship with a person or thing: *two sisters unable to relate to each other.*

I learned the hard way through one of the first speeches I gave during speech training what it is to know my audience. It was an outstanding example of understanding your ideal client. This alone will save you time and the frustration that comes from not telling your story effectively.

I was scheduled to speak to an audience. As I was determining what to speak about, I came up with the idea that centered around the time of year. In fact, the day of my speech was the start of the NCAA college basketball tournament. I thought, perfect; I will twist a play on words around the tourney, and the crowd will love it.

My speech title was *Bracket Domination.*

I put an opening together naming a majority of the mascots (Wildcats, Tigers and Bruins...oh my) that would be participating in the tournament. I quickly focused in on one individual in the back of the room. He was smiling and nodding at each ingenious way I introduced a team. Because of his reaction, I thought I was wowing the audience.

As I moved into the next part of my speech, I guided the audience through the techniques and strategies that must be used in order to dominate your bracket. I described how to use a very scientific analysis of team records and the strength of schedule played to make your choices. I even gave an example of making your pick based on your favorite place to visit.

I closed up the presentation with, "let's go out and be Bracket Dominator's this year."

I was feeling good about the delivery and how I had done. Feeding off the vibes I received from a few in the audience, I sat down confident that my message had been heard by all.

In this particular group, they have someone from the audience, which gives an evaluation of the speech. It was at this point that I learned the importance of knowing your audience. They opened, "It was a good speech, but I didn't know what you were talking about until halfway through your speech." My heart sank when I heard those words. They continued, "The picture that I had in my head was a bracket that you use to hold a bookcase together. I was, therefore, confused as to why you were describing animals. The two didn't fit. I looked around and others seemed to be getting it. What was I missing, I began to wonder?"

Wow. Talk about having your bubble popped.

It was one of the most important lessons that I have learned. I didn't consider that there might be listeners in the audience who didn't share my particular interests and who thus wouldn't be knowledgeable of my chosen subject matter.

A little more preparation and thought on my part would have stopped this embarrassing moment. If I had taken the time to be less focused on myself and more focused on my audience, I would have crafted a story understandable to anyone in my audience. The use of a story will allow you to relate your message to a broader demographic, gender, or cultural group.

What if I had open with a scene from a story in kids' lives around the country? Something like:

> *The basketball bounced back into their hand off the pavement. They took a deep breath of air. Then called out the countdown of the clock as they dribble around the defender, which happened to be a Chevy. At the front bumper they stopped and shoot, just before the imaginary clock called out zero.*
>
> *Ladies and gentleman, have you seen a child play out a similar situation in a movie, TV show, or even your back yard...*

A scene like this would have allowed the audience to start to paint their picture. If they had experienced or seen this scene before, their sub-conscious mind would have gone back and pulled this memory.

How?

What kind of Chevy did they dribble past?

Was it mine or one that your brain brought back to memory?

For me it was my old 1973 light blue, rust bomb Chevy Nova, with two red passenger doors.

It was an important factor I learned when listening to Randy Harvey, 2002 World Champion of Public Speaking, give a presentation. He taught how to draw the contour of the object or person and allow the listening audience to fill in the details. It is how you make a story relatable. The story is their story.

Will they not relate to their own story better than to the story someone else?

If I had done this in that speech, I would have allowed this listener to paint their own picture. They would have taken ownership of the story, because they found features and factors of which they could take ownership. The story you tell your audience must be crafted in a way that allows them to connect and relate to it.

Imagine that the evaluator of my speech above was an ideal prospect who had found us on the internet. Would they have stayed to listen to the whole message?

DOUG KLIEWER

Probably not.

It would be more likely that they would have clicked off and moved on to a different website, and found a solution to the problem they were trying to solve. The opportunity to connect would have been lost.

As Eugene H. Peterson in his book, *The Message Remix,* says, "That's why I tell stories: to create readiness, to nudge the people toward receptive insight. In their present state, they can stare till doomsday and not see it, listen till they're blue in the face and not get it." The story that we are telling must be relatable.

Stories allow you to show your openness. It is this nakedness of sorts that allow the listener to relate on a much deeper level than blasting them with feature after feature of the widget. You see, telling your story is not about you. The story is about the experience of your audiences, about their connection to your story.

Making a story relatable is about allowing the bride-to-be to come into your salon and imagine herself in the perfect dress and makeup for her special day. She has to see herself living out her story. If able to picture herself walking down the aisle looking beautiful, she will feel connected to the story. If not, then she will keep looking until she has that connection.

Make your story relatable to your audience. If you are marketing to an older audience, then you must use familiar terms connected to their experience in a real way. If your target market is female, then use stories into which they can place themselves.

It is this relation to a personal situation that will allow your audience to connect with you faster and deeper. It is why you must tell a story and make it relatable. Once a story is relatable, we then make it compelling. Let's go see how.

MAKE IT COMPELLING

"Move your listeners' hearts and their feet and wallet will follow"

---Paul Guber

"History is full of blank spaces, but good stories, invariably, are not."

---Sara Sheridan

Let me share part of a recent speech that I heard at a Toastmasters meeting. Toastmaster Sheryl Cox shared with the audience a story about her son, Benjamin, who, born with cerebral palsy, has from day one had to deal with the symptoms of an incredibly debilitating disease. The objective assigned to her for this speech was to use logic and emotion to persuade listeners to adopt her perspective and take action. We will pick it up, part way through her speech:

Benjamin and I were walking in a park one day. As we walked, we noticed there was a baseball game going on. Benjamin asked, "Mom, could I play?" I was a little nervous with his request, but not one to limit my son's activities because of his disability; I approached the team.

DOUG KLIEWER

I asked one of the boys if Ben could play. "Well, we're losing by 6 and its the 8th inning, so why not," grudgingly one of the boys said.

Benjamin was ecstatic! He went and plopped himself down on the bench. They even found an extra uniform for him to put on. I stood on the sidelines, and a small tear of joy trickled down my cheek. The team finished the 8th inning still down in the game.

To start the top of the 9th inning, the team put Ben in right field. There were no balls hit to him during that half of the inning, but the smile on his face said it all. He was just so excited to be out there.

The bottom of the 9th and the boys were still down by four runs. Then they started to hit the ball and get on the base and score. They loaded the bases. There were two outs and the tying run was on the second. Ben was the next scheduled batter. Now the boys had a decision to make.

Do they send up a pitch hitter for Ben and keep their hopes of winning this game?

Or, do they allow Ben to hit and give up on winning the game?

To my shock, they sent Ben up to bat. Encouraging him to go up there and get a hit.

The pitcher from the other team looked around him at the bases all full, as he stood on the mound. He gets this one easy out, and they win the game. He glanced one more time around the field, and then he took a couple of steps closer to Ben and gave him a gentle underhand toss.

STORYTELLING 2 SUCCESS

Ben swung with all his might. He missed. Strike one was called out.

After getting the ball back, the pitcher...took a couple of more steps toward Ben and tossed the ball even softer than the first time.

Ben started his swing and hit the ball. My heart filled with ardor at the hit.

The ball went right back to the pitcher. He picked it up. Game was over.

But the pitcher reached back and threw the ball hard and high above the first baseman, so that there was no way he could catch it.

The team started screaming at Ben. "Run! Ben, run!"

Ben startled, started to run toward 1st base and stepped on it as the rest of the baserunners began to make their way toward home.

"Run to second, Ben," came the scream from the bench as ball still lies in foul territory. Ben started to go toward second. The right fielder picked up the ball. And he also reached back and gave the ball a heave way over the second baseman head.

As Ben now stood on second the shortstop pointed to third and helps guide Ben toward it. The whole team was up against the dugout. Jumping up and down and screaming, "Run, Ben run."

By this time the whole crowd of parents, grandparents, siblings, and friends that had gathered to watch the game, were also standing and yelling, "Run, Ben run."

The team rushed from the dugout and was waiting at home plate as Ben stepped on it.

What will you do when faced with a decision of winning or losing a game, or lifting up someone to be the hero of the game?

What a story. Flannery O'Conner in her book, M*ystery and Manners: Occasional Prose* states well what this story was able to do to the audience that day, "There is something in us, as storytellers and as listeners to stories that require the redemptive act. A demand that what falls is offered the chance to be restored."

Sheryl's story of her son is a perfect example of what each one of us must bring into our storytelling. In order to make a story compelling we must engage with our customers on a soul level. As Akash Karia, TED Talks Storytelling, puts it, "That's just one of the advantages of stories - they allow you to share your message without your audience feeling like you're preaching to them, which in turn makes it easier for them to accept your message."

Did you see how the story crafted around a hero's journey? The speaker in this case drew us in by engaging the antagonist with our hero. As Ryan Avery says, "challenge your protagonist with a worthy opponent."

Who or maybe what was the antagonist in the story we read above?

This is where the art of storytelling comes into play. Different viewers may have completely different responses to a painting by Van Gogh. Similarly, various people may arrive at very different meanings for our characters in this story.

The antagonist could have been the cerebral palsy or any of the boys on the team or the pitcher or right fielder. Each of these characters had opportunities to hinder the hero on his or her journey. Did you see others?

Each one of us will read or listen to the story above and bring into it our experiences, past generational influences, and culture we live in today. As we mentioned several chapters earlier, this is where the connection happens. When we can place ourselves inside the story that we are hearing or reading, this is where you will start to see faster and deeper connections.

As a business individual, is that not what you want with your customers and prospects? If we can create these compelling hero stories and use them as strategies in our business, we also can create this connection. Your client only gets value when they plug into the light socket of your business.

Now comes an important aspect of storytelling that will revolutionize your business. It is one slight movement that will take the already dominant keys we have learned of the story and put them in overdrive for your business. Let's learn the Hero Maker Blueprint.

CHAPTER 5

THE HERO MAKER BLUEPRINT

> "There is no greater agony than bearing an untold story inside you."
>
> --Maya Angelou

I want to take you through a quick exercise that is going to help us start crafting the most important type of story we need to be sharing. Take a moment to think back over the last six months, and the customer(s) that you have met. Maybe you need to open your CRM or review your calendar to prompt you. Do you have the names and faces of these clients or prospects?

Next, I want you narrow it down to the person who was in a desperate state, or most desperate state, to solve a problem in an area where you are a specialist. Because it fit perfectly, your specialty or widget created an element of relief.

When they called you, how did the conversation go? Did you hear the crack in their voice as they explained what was happening in their life? Did they plead with you to help? Was there some urgency?

I remember receiving a voicemail from a realtor client of mine, when I was selling home insurance. The message began, "Is there any way you can...?" I knew it was a dire situation when my cell phone went off repeatedly as I was listened to the voicemail.

I quickly called him back. The fast pace of his voice expressed that he needed something done yesterday. He explained he had a home buyer who was going to close that next day and hadn't purchased a homeowner insurance policy. To add kindling to the fire, the new homeowner was moving into the new home the day of closing, because they had to move out of their current residence. The moving truck was loaded. If didn't close that next day, they would push back the closing 2 days. "Is there ANY WAY you can please help them out?"

Now maybe the client you helped didn't have quite the same urgency or maybe it was much more. Do you have your person captured in your mind?

What happened with your client?

Were you able to solve the problem or better yet show them how to solve this problem? I assume because this memory is fresh in your mind, that something positive came out of the incident.

Now take a moment and start to relive everything that took place. Connect to the emotional state of the client when you first met with them. How did it change through the process? What was the difference in their emotions after their experience with you and your business?

Let me ask you, "Can you tell this specific client story to someone right now?"

Yes!

Why?

When you tell a story about a customer, you describe how and where they were when you first entered into their story. You detail what you know and what took place to get them to this situation. You have been there, and your subconscious mind is pulling from these memories. And as Craig Valentine, Toastmaster World Champion 1999, puts it, "You've got to invite them into the scene of your story so they can hear it how you heard it, see it how you saw it, and feel how you felt it." By this process, you bring life into your client's story.

What does this do for the listener? You open the door to a person to whom they can relate their lives. It is easier for them to transpose their lives and their problems onto another client.

Here is a nugget of truth that you cannot miss. In a business relationship, you, as a business, are viewed by the client as being on a different level—usually some level above them. But when you bring in another client who they view as being on their own level, you show them just how important connection is to you.

You have a created a partnership with your client's story. This partner will in effect bridge the gap between two worlds by aligning itself with both. On the one hand, the partner (i.e. character from the story) aligns with the world of the prospect as someone who has walked in their shoes and experienced their problems. The prospect finds it easy to relate to him/her. On the other hand, the hero of your story is also connected to your business and to your world by virtue of being an actual client. So he/she is aligned with you also. Aligned with both, the client hero from your story naturally bridges whatever gap may exist (in the prospect's mind) between you and the prospect.

My above realtor client and their clients became a bridge for my insurance business to express our story of going over and above the norm, as we told how the home buyer received the homeowner policy in time to complete the close. They moved into their new home without having to unload the truck twice.

It is an integral part of human nature to connect. But as we discussed in earlier chapters, this desire is many times overridden with a fight or flight mentality. Your clients and prospects want to join to someone to whom they can relate themselves in their own world. It is where they will always want to connect. It is safe. It is comfortable. It is familiar. It is why the Hero Maker Blueprint will show you how to form this connection for them and get them to stay and listen.

But what is the Hero Maker Blueprint you ask?

The Hero Maker Blueprint

The Hero Maker Blueprint in its simplest form is the process of telling a story where your client is the hero of the story. It is a matter of taking the above client story you just created and sharing it with your clients and prospects. It is the story that will describe to anyone who hears it, what your business is about.

Here is the key point: The client is the HERO. When this client is the hero of your business story, then you will connect deeper and faster with other clients and prospects.

There is a sacrifice of ego that is going to happen. The story is not about the years and years of training that you did, but it is about how the client used those years of training. The story is not about the sweat and blood you spilled to solve a problem, but about how the client used their own effort to solve their problem.

I can hear some of you saying to yourself, "I must be the hero?" Yes, they are coming to you to solve a problem, but they are true hero.

I had those same thoughts. In today's world of escalating certain individuals to a different status by turning them into stars or superheroes, it is easy to get sucked into that trap. I now need share a life changing "Aha" moment before we get into the details of the Hero Maker Blueprint.

HAVE YOU HAD AN AHA?

"We make our lives bigger or smaller, more expansive or more limited, according to the interpretation of life that is our story."

---Christina Baldwin,
Storycatcher: Making Sense of Our Lives through the Power and Practice of Story

This year I started to train to earn the right to represent the local district of Toastmasters at the World Championship of Public Speaking. The district makes up pretty much the whole state of Michigan, minus Detroit. I hired a coach, Chelsea Avery, to help with this daunting and yet exciting challenge. After putting multiple hours into preparing my speech for the first stage of the competition, I presented it to a group as a practice run. I sent her a copy of the transcript and video recording of that practice run to Chelsea.

Now Chelsea brings a unique perspective and is the reason that I asked her to coach me. Her husband, Ryan, had won the World Championship of Public Speaking in 2012. In the process they followed to achieve this title, they had discovered a small nugget that separated the winners from the rest.

So, after listening to the video and reading my first draft, she asked me, "Who is the hero of your speech right now?"

I thought for a moment and then stated, "Well I want to teach the audience how to love better. It was a problem for me, and I had to learn the hard way how to love better. I want to tell the audience what I learned and help them do it better."

Her reply, "So, you are the hero of your story?"

"Yeah, I guess."

She went on, "Let me ask you, who the audience, at some deep level, wants the hero to be?

I went silent, because I didn't know.

She then let the cat out of the bag metaphorically speaking, "Themselves." "You need to show your audience how they can become a hero."

My audience wanted to be a hero.

It was at that moment that I realized that in order to relate to my audience. I had to put myself as a "speaker" at a level where they could insert themselves as the hero of this story. I now knew that my audience wanted to be a hero. They were the ones that wanted to solve the problem that lay there in front of them. All they needed was someone to teach them how to do it. They needed a mentor to show them how to be a hero.

In the previous chapter, I gave a section of my speech about my daughter. Who was the teacher or mentor?

Here it is again and see if you can catch who it is:

As I extended my hand to my daughter, my mind raced back to the future, in a Michael J Fox Delorean time machine to...

March, 2000. I was in my chair in awe of the little present nestled on my chest. Her knees tucked up under, her little bottom...pointed in the air. The scent of baby shampoo gently lifted from her full head of hair. A sight that would make any balding man jealous.

My father was there in his coke bottle glasses and suspenders to impart his wisdom

"Son, she looks innocent now, but there's this thing called teenager. Remember, Love never gives up...and whoa that's a lotta hair."

STORYTELLING 2 SUCCESS

Being a new dad was great. The next three years were spent reading bedtime stories, coloring princesses and changing stinky diapers

There was one day when my wife's panicked voice pierced through our home.

"I can't find Corrin! She was in the sandbox. And now she's gone."

We frantically looked in every nook and cranny.

Hopes of we'll find her, soon faded to worry, and then collapsed into sheer...terror

The woods?

Out the door, I flew...like Carl Lewis

As I rounded the bend, I saw...pig tails bobbing up and down running toward me, ecstatic to show me the stash she had found.

I scooped her up; she squealed.

I kissed her raspberry stained cheeks.

She placed one of her prized possessions in my mouth. My taste buds erupted with fresh out of the oven, raspberry pie, ala mode and a prickly stem.

Later that night talking with my father, he said, "You learned in your searching, that Love never gives up...and you did save me a piece of the pie?"

Who was the mentor of my story?

It was my father. He was the person who taught me how to love better. Or better stated, my father was the one who taught us how to love better.

Why did I say us?

How do I get the audience to look at me as an equal to them? As was referenced earlier, the prospect (i.e. audience in this section) is on a different level or in another world. If I just come out as speaker and tell them they need to love better, they will naturally resist the idea. They will naturally disengage from my message because I am metaphorically talking down to them, telling them what to do, as it were. But by introducing into the story a mentor whom I revere, the audience naturally identifies with me as student and therefore willingly joins in with me to listen to my father's instruction. By introducing my father as mentor, I in essence I pull up a chair alongside the audience as we all sit together absorbing my father's message of love.

What Chelsea wanted me to see and communicate is the importance of my father as guide in this speech. It is the same for us. What we do with the Hero Maker Blueprint is tell a story where we as business owner become mentor to the hero. The hero is the client.

Let's think about this in a business setting. When you want to introduce a message that is accepted by the audience, who does this best?

Is it the client or you as business owner? Client, correct?

The prospect (e.g. audience) wants to be the hero who solves the problem in their own story, but they need someone to teach them the required steps.

So you tell a story where your client listened to your instruction and by acting on it solved the problem lying before them. The prospect connects with the client who is the bridge to the message you are teaching. You as business owner are now sharing through your client hero. You are not standing over and/or talking down.

Implementing teaching into our marketing creates a conjoining of two worlds, your prospects world and your business world. There is power in two versus one.

The power of teaching is with a mentor, and the power of connection to the audience is with the hero. It is the combination of these two dynamics that will transform a good story into a great story. And it is the blending of these two powerful characters in storytelling that will push your business ahead of your competitions. As business owner, when we elevate our client to the place of central character in our story and show our relationship to them as mentor, we create an incredibly powerful connection to them. It is this connection that we then use to grow and nurture our business relationship.

We must as business professionals check our egos at the door. A business person as mentor will place themselves in the background. It is a conscious effort to ascend our clients to heroes and put them on a pedestal of sorts for everyone to see. We then as business owner are allowed to teach, create, and manifest new heroes for our business. By this manifestation, we assemble a stronger foundation for our company to continue to grow and prosper.

Questions they ask

Let's go back to your client story which we started to assemble at the beginning of the chapter. You have your client who had a dilemma, and they came to you for assistance. Through the process, you then helped them to overcome this issue. Then as you start to retell this story to current clients or potential customers there are a couple of questions going through their heads as they listen to this Hero Maker Blueprint story:

You have a client like me?

They have the same problem as I do, because I didn't think that anyone else had this same problem?

You were able to help them solve this problem that both of us have?

Wait a minute, you showed them how to be the hero of their story?

Can you do the same for me?

I was helping a client communicate an aspect of his business to his own clients and potential customers. We were working on shooting a video to use as a means of communication. The setting of the shoot was a beautiful home on a large river in our area. The day was gorgeous even if slightly overcast. Every once in awhile the sun would poke from behind the clouds and sparkle off the water. The shoot was happening in the dining room overlooking the tranquil body of flowing water.

As the client was relating his story in the video, he suddenly experienced difficulty describing just how the buying process works for his clients. We stopped and I asked him "Is there a client who just went through this process?" He quickly said, "Yes." "Okay," I said, "Let's start shooting again, and I want you to tell me about that experience."

His breath slowed, and we shot the video in one take from there. It was fun to watch as the story flowed off his lips. You could tell that his client was appreciative of the work he had done. You could physically sense it. It was like all the tension we had experienced moments earlier was released out over the water.

Now when a new buyer sees this video that we created, they will be able to find the answers to those questions we listed above. There will be that attraction to learn how they can also become a hero. Let's go now to the Hero Maker Blueprint.

Hero Maker Blueprint

I have created a diagram to help us see the arc along which we want to move our story. You will see it on the next page.

Hero Maker Blueprint

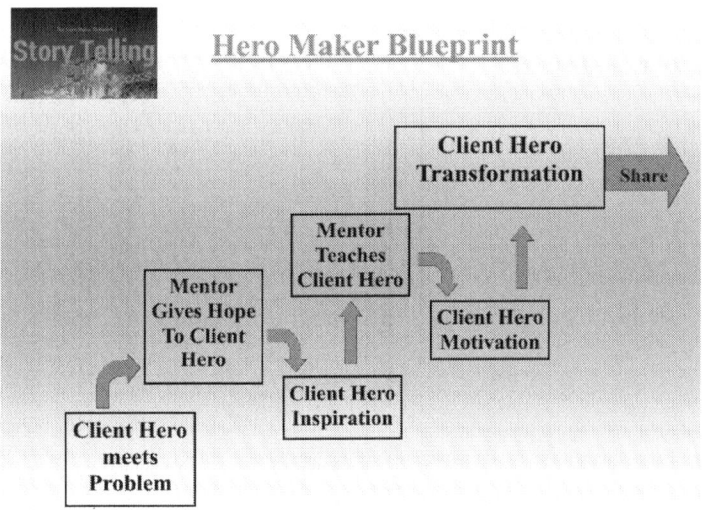

Each story we read has a particular arc to it. Similarly, the heroic stories you create and share will follow an arc determined by the Hero Maker Blueprint. To me it is the most powerful of all marketing ideas out there, this idea of making heroes out of your clients, showing and mentoring them on how to solve challenges that present themselves, walking them through the dark tunnel of a difficult problem and seeing them emerge on the other side a victor, a solutions engineer. Let's work through the Hero Maker Blueprint.

LEARN TO LIKE PROBLEMS

"If you want meaning for your brand or company, dare to embrace conflict"

---Antonio Nunez Lopez,

Do you like problems?

As we have stated earlier, the beginning of your client's story is that they have a problem that needs solving. They need a pipe fixed under the sink, or they have injured their back. Your clients also face the potential for problems that could impact their future. Perhaps they need to protect their assets from someone or something so that their loved ones will receive the best care.

Do you like problems? No, we don't like problems or inconvenience. We do everything in our power to remove or protect ourselves from them. Our clients or prospects are no different.

But as a business owner we need to learn how to love problems. Problems keep us in business, because if there weren't problems we wouldn't have a business.

I had a client relate how a prospective buyer had approached them for their services, describing exactly they needed. My client responded, "That shouldn't be a problem. I know what you are looking for and can get it for you." Then my client asked, "When do you need this?"

The buyer said, "In two weeks."

My client thought, now that's a problem!

You see, my client's normal process of ordering and receiving from the manufacturer is 4-6 weeks. This person needed it in 2 weeks. It was a serious problem for the customer, and it was causing incredible stress in their lives. They needed relief from the pressure and fast. So my client was presented with an opportunity but also a problem: do they deliver service in a way that adds to the pressure of the buyer or in a way that also provides hope and perhaps ameliorates the buyer's anxiety.

HOPE FOR

"Everything that is done in the world is done by hope."

---Martin Luther

Hope is what we need

When sitting down and talking with business owners over the years, I have heard many stories detailing concerns about how their businesses were doing. I was sitting in the office of one specific client during the last economic downturn in 2008-2009.

It was towards the end of a Friday and everyone else had left for the weekend. As we walked up to his office, I noticed that all of the desks were neatly arranged. I mean all of them. Now some individuals are very tidy and keep their desks clear of clutter at all costs. But there are some of us (yes, me included) that are clutter challenged. But each and every desk lay spotless. The discussion that evening was centered on how the business was performing during this difficult time. I remember him saying as he looked out into the shop, "We have work, right, that will keep us busy for a few weeks. We are out bidding on more jobs, but more and more firms are coming from other cities trying to find work." He paused, then looked straight at me, "I hope we can get a couple of jobs, so I can hire back some of my laid off employees."

Hope is that emotion we cling to when the future is unknown. It can begin in a pretty dark place. It might begin with a feeling by some character, for example, that life has thrown a curve ball and that they are left with nothing more than their own cognitive abilities for forging a solution to the problem.

This part of a story can be a lonely place for the character(s). How many times does a movie move the main character to a place where they are all alone? No one is around to help them. The menacing antagonist is closing in. What are they to do?

Without hope that they can overcome the problem, the character or prospect will become inactive. We talked about fight or flight earlier. But another core instinct is to freeze. This may be beneficial for the short term in order to assess the situation. But being sedentary for too long is not good. In fact it is unhealthy, harmful for the individual that has the problem and ultimately for the business that has the solution to the problem. As Luther well understood, life would stop if there wasn't a hope.

How can we as a business provide hope to those seeking our services? A business needs to relay confidence to a client and/or prospect by illustrating from their own business history that "this issue has been resolved before and now it can be resolved once again". The prospect then begins to see that there is a light in the midst of their imagined dark tunnel.

Back in chapter 3 I introduced you to a friend of mine whose daughter has Rett syndrome. He was telling once how being a parent of a Rett child can be a lonely place. There are not many people who understand the situation and or even want to take the time to learn about these precious little angels.

For example, Rett girls for the most part do not have the capacity to communicate with words. But as my friend has taught me, they use their eyes to communicate. A frequent source of frustration and consequentially of acting out, however, is that they have not been given adequate time to answer a question asked of them. You see, they take 10-15 or more seconds to answer one question.

What is your reaction if your child doesn't answer your question in 2 seconds? You ask it again, because you think they didn't hear you, which sometimes may be true. A Rett girl, however, will hear you and be processing the answer but just needs time to communicate it. So if the question is asked again and again, they continually have to reprocess it, which in turn becomes overwhelming to them. Now it is easy to understand why a Rett girl might experience frustration. But can you also see why a parent may feel lonely in this kind of situation?

But my friend has journeyed valiantly through his own place of loneliness and despair. And by remembering that loneliness, he is actively reaching out to other Rett dads to walk beside them as a beacon of hope.

Why? Because he knows what it is like to think no one is there who can care and understand. But he did find someone was there to help him, and now he uses his story to connect with other dads with the same message of hope.

Hope begins as a seed planted in the soil of our mind. Hope is a life of possibility overcoming predicament.

Let's go back and illustrate this with a business. Remember the client story earlier, which needed someone willing to fulfill an order in one third of the time it normally takes. The hope my client brought to this prospective buyer moved them from despair. No matter how faint, a little glimmer of light became visible in their dark world. So the seed of hope can be the placement of a small client hero story within the story being told.

In other words, as you are telling future prospect **A** the client hero story of buyer **B** who needed the order done in two weeks, you add in client **C** to your story.

Who is client **C**? Client C is the client hero you introduced to client B to give them hope. After client C perhaps you also begin to stack up wow experiences from other previous clients who have successfully used your mentoring to overcome a dilemma. Each added story illustrates strength and confidence that there are more heroes out there and this resolution has been accomplished repeated times. Hope now turns into a growing beam of light feed not only by the testimonial of client C but also by the testimonials of clients D, E and F. As we provide hope in this way from our treasure chest of client hero stories, it opens the door for prospect A to start their own journey out of their impasse.

INSPIRE THEM TO OVERCOME

"Story is a yearning meeting an obstacle."

--Robert Olen Butler

Inspiring your client hero is the next step in our Hero Maker Blueprint. The hope you and I bring to the client hero is a description of a past action by another. There is still some work that needs to be done in order for our client hero to take ownership.

Inspiration is the change in thinking for our client hero. Our client B approached us with the belief that there was nothing that anyone could do to solve the two-week order dilemma. Now we have introduced them to client C or made a promise that shows there is a ray of light. Inspiration is to be in spirit with this other character. They are in step and attach themselves to this changed idea that something is getting done. It is the deep emotion of kindred spirit.

In the progression of our client hero story, client B enacts an internal change in attitude from complete anxiety and pessimism to the belief their problem can be handled and solved. There is past proof if need be. They now have hope and inspiration. Now our mentor/business professional must motivate our client hero to take action.

GET THEM MOVING

"The only thing standing between you and your goal is the bullshit story you keep telling yourself as to why you can't achieve,"

---Jordan Belfort

Hope and inspiration are wonderful feelings that we all can marry ourselves into. But at some point there must be action. The next progression of our client hero is that they must be motivated to move into the unknown. Our client hero must decide to take action. Motivation on many levels will bring some sacrifice on their part. All heroes have sacrificed something in order to get where they are.

The client we have been discussing had to sacrifice some extra money in order for the product to arrive at a quicker pace than normal. This escalation of production cost more. The client was willing to sacrifice something in order to receive their purchase in two weeks.

Remember an earlier point that we don't like problems. If we don't like problems, then we avoid sacrifice. Why? Sacrifice involves a death to something. Not a physical death, but a monetary death or the death of freedoms. But in order to come out the other side a hero, we as mentors must motivate our client to sacrifice. There is a giving up that happens. There is a trust...a faith in our mentor.

We as mentors/business professionals accompany the hero only to the point where they need our support: into the unknown territory on the road of misery and from there to the point just before he passes through this affliction. The idea, perhaps, is that the hero has progressed in the evolution of his awareness. He no longer needs magical help from an external source. He's found the spirit within himself.

I don't, however, feel that this always reflects the way it works in the process of change. We certainly grow less dependent on our helpers when we cross the return threshold, but helpers are always coming in and out of our lives, whether directly or indirectly. I think this is an important point to emphasize because we need to cherish our helpers, whoever or whatever they are, throughout our lives. They further inspire us to be helpers to others.

I remember certain clients from my financial advising business repeatedly using this kind of language to describe their feelings. They knew that in order for them to be able to retire, they would have to sacrifice some today in order to experience later. My clients decided not to go on extravagant vacations. They went out to eat less frequently. Each one of these sacrifices was a death to something. But in the process they transformed their motivation into a successful retirement, where now they have a nest egg accumulated to take an expensive vacation or two.

As Maya Angelou once said, "We delight in the beauty of the butterfly but rarely admit the changes it has gone through to achieve that beauty." We as mentors must motive our client hero to embrace the fact that in order for them to become butterflies of something new and different, they will need to make sacrifices along the way.

TRANSFORMATION...HAPPENS

> "Scared and sacred are spelled with the same letters. Awful proceeds from the same root word as awesome. Terrify and terrific. Every negative experience holds the seed of transformation."
>
> ---Alan Cohen

Like a seed of hope planted in the soil, our client hero with the proper watering of inspiration and motivation will explode from the ground as a new life form open to the sunshine of possibility.

This genesis of sorts is the transformational success.

As Donald Miller from his book, *A Million Miles in a Thousand Year: What I learned Editing my Life*, eloquently puts it,

> "If the point of life is the same as the point of a story, the point of life is character transformation. If I got any comfort as I set out on my first story, it was that in nearly every story, the protagonist is transformed. He's a jerk at the beginning and nice at the end, or a coward at the beginning and brave at the end. If the character doesn't change, the story hasn't happened yet. And if story is derived from real life, if story is just condensed version of life then life itself may be designed to change us so that we evolve from one kind of person to another."

What evolved with my client is that they were able to fill a purchase order in the two-week timeframe. Their client had transformed from a depressed state of no hope into a state of expectant successes. This client of mine and then also, their customer looked at problems and sacrifices as not something to fear, but as a necessary step on the journey of success. The connection that these two individuals had to each other was strong. And would get stronger and stronger the more that journeyed. They had a hero story to share now.

We produce a story that centers around this hero creation. And as the story unfolds before the viewer, they find it much easier to place themselves as a character into the story as well. As was mentioned earlier, these questions start to develop in their subconscious,

"Is it possible for me to be this hero?"

Or "If I went through these steps, could I see the same kind of successes that this Hero is experiencing?"

"Will this business owner also promote my success to the world to see?"

Where the power continues to grow is when they build upon their Hero's success and find or create ways to take your widget to new levels not even you could have expected. Reach out to your clients and get to know how some of the things you've done for them have changed their lives for the better. Then go and promote them to the world. It will help your customer. It will help you. It will incredibly help the person who watches this story unfold, as it inspires them to bigger and greater things. It will become their transformational success. It will become a new story which you then can produce to bring a New Hero to the world.

Throw the celebration party of the century!

CHAPTER 6

CELEBRATE TRANSFORMATIONAL SUCCESS OF HERO'S

> "When we quit thinking primarily about ourselves and our self-preservation, we undergo a truly heroic transformation of consciousness."
>
> Joseph Campbell

Why is celebrating your clients transformational success beneficial to you? In order to be in business you need to sell to clients. There has to be a sale at some point, otherwise you have nothing. So if you want to build a business that will last, you will need to strengthen your position with your clientele and also bring in additional clients.

As a business owner, one of the most connective ways to promote your business is to portray a current client and the success they've had by working with you. A simple breakdown is: what you did to bring about your client's success and how you helped them transition from problem stage to solution stage. You do this by bringing in and celebrating your customer's transformational success: you tell a Client Hero Story. What better way to advertise your own story as a business than to tell the stories of your clients? They have been able to experience something which has changed them and made them better or put them into a better place. Observe that moment with them in a narrative. Be excited for them in a story. Explain to the world that these are your own heroes. After all, they are the ones who have made you successful; they are your success.

The last step of our Hero Maker Blueprint is to share your hero with the world. Hopefully by now the evolution of the story has brought you through enough surrenders that this last surrender becomes easy. The culmination is placement of the "Medal of Hero" on your client.

You make them the stars of your business. And by making them the heroes you in turn relay a message which is at the core of who you are as a business and as a person, namely, that it's not solely about you but also about helping other individuals or businesses solve problems.

Isn't the purpose of your business to provide goods/services which help customers solve problems or enrich their lives in other ways? Then what better way is there to promote your business than by promoting a client?

Client testimonials are business promotions on steroids. You display to a potential prospect that you were able to help a client, how they changed because of the experience or service you provided. Maybe you display how your product helped a client lose weight, work faster, be more productive, save money or even make more money. What happens during this metamorphosis of sorts a hero has been created from the tribe of life

Let me ask you, "Do you want your client or customer to use your widget and experience pain?"

No!!

If we have a business that is seeking to thrive and be sustainable, not only today but also tomorrow, then we need our customers to experience something good from their interaction with us and/or our widget. Shouldn't we become ecstatic for their success?

Yes!!

How powerful would the story of your business be by putting these successes on display? You can take this power to the nth degree by moving the focus from the widget, or even from you and your business, to the real hero, your client.

Aren't they the real hero?

Nancy Duarte, author of *Resonate: Present Visual Stories that Transform Audience,* says "humans are obsessed with transformation, maybe because we live on an earth that transforms with four seasons and cycles of birth, life and death. People love to observe story and transformation. It humanizes and connects us."

They trusted what you were saying or selling. They are the ones who should be celebrated!

Do you want your business to grow? Do you want it to continue to grow?

Your business grows because your customer continues to be successful by using your widget. When you promote this success, it shows a prospective buyer in a tangible way that what you are selling is working. Here is the paradigm shift that must take place. Your success must not be your success, but the ride on the shirttails of your customer and their success with your widget.

We produce a story that centers around this hero creation. And as the story unfolds, it becomes easy for a prospect to place themselves as a character in this story as well. A question starts to develop in their subconscious, "is it possible for me to be this hero," or "what if I went through these steps, could I see the same kind of successes that this Hero is experiencing?" Then as the question even matures—"Would this business owner also promote my success to the world to see?" —the prospect suddenly becomes empowered, because they not only imagine possibilities but also identify with them by imagining what (consequences) might follow were those possibilities to be actualized.

This is the creation of hope, since the prospect now forms a path in their mind of what the future may hold for them. The full power of the story will ultimately become manifest when the prospect formulates a course of action based upon your Hero story and then eventually uses their own actions to take your widget to new levels even you could not have expected.

Let's recap our Hero Maker Blueprint principal components and illustrate with a story:

Hope for...

Why do we hope? Or what do we wish to happen? Isn't it usually a feeling to have something that is better than our current state?

I wish my current state of hunger to go away.

I hope I can find a home where my family can grow and be safe.

I hope that this pain in my back will go away.

I hope my business would grow.

Hope. We all have a feeling of hope that we experience throughout our lives. When we first meet our customers, they have a hope that is driving them to find a resolution to the dilemma in which they find themselves.

Inspire them to overcome

The next step our hero will go through is the inspiration to do something. Remember that our primary action is to either fight or flight. When a problem comes into our hero's life, this problem along with the mentor's help becomes the inspiration to do something. It prompts or "internally pushes" the hero to figure out some way to move from the tension. Here is a story to form a skeletal picture of how a client hero story might look.

> *I am part of the 2 Success Mastermind group. We are a group of like-minded business owners and professionals that meet every couple of weeks to help each other with the successes of our businesses. Catherine, an estate planning attorney in the group, was sharing about a client, a set of parents, whose daughter had encountered a medical issue while away to college and had to be admitted to a hospital.*

After admission the parents called the hospital, seeking information about their daughter's condition. However, due to new healthcare laws the hospital would not release any medical information to them, because their daughter was now a legal adult and because the hospital had no consent forms on file to cover such a release. Frantic at what was transpiring, they called Catherine. She reminded them that they had previously assembled a Medial Power of Attorney for their daughter. Relieved that the situation had already been resolved, due to Catherine's foresight, of course, the client immediately faxed the necessary papers to the hospital and thus were able receive updates about their daughter's status and be part of her decision-making process. As a result they were able to help their daughter receive the best treatment available.

What was interesting is that another member, Janis, stood up a couple of weeks later and added to the above story. She said, "After I had heard Catherine describing what had happened, I thought, my son just turned 18 years old. What if something were to happen to him?"

So what we have here is a business owner sharing a client hero story, which in turn motivates a listener of that story to initiate their own journey toward becoming a hero in someone's story.

Get them moving

The next evolution your Hero Maker Story will go through is motivation. We can have all the inspiration we want, but unless we finally put legs under that inspiration it will remain nothing more than a warm feeling. Let's continue Janis' story above from my mastermind group.

Hearing Catherine's Hero Maker story, she arranged to get the Medical Power of Attorney paperwork done for her son. Now if her son injured himself while playing a sport or in an accident while away at college, she would be able to help in his medical decision-making process.

Transformation happens before your eyes.

What Janis said next showed the progression from anxiety to appreciativeness.

"As a parent it was such a peace of mind, knowing that if something were to happen to my son, my husband and I would not be in the dark or unable to help."

Did you see how the hero finds the means or resources to resolve the tension? What is the result? It is a transformation to something peaceful.

They don't keep it to themselves

The result, if you use the Hero Maker Blueprint, is that the hero wants to share their story. They want to encourage others to be mentored by the Hero Maker so they can help them be heroes as well. I have heard multiple times in different settings stories similar to that of Janis, how, connecting to a problem in someone else's story and inspired to take action, this or that person was able to transform their own state of mind into something more peaceful.

I don't, however, feel that this always reflects the way it works in the process of change. We certainly grow less dependent on our helpers as we cross certain thresholds. But helpers are always coming in and out of our lives, whether directly or indirectly. I think this is an important point to emphasize because we need to cherish our helpers, whoever or whatever they are, throughout our lives. They further inspire us to be helpers to others.

You want to strengthen a business? Then the Hero Maker Blueprint is the means by which you will be able to do it. The blueprint will build it, but you still need to tell it.

CHAPTER 7

TELL A CLIENT HERO STORY

"Great stories happen to those who can tell them."

--Ira Glas

I think that this quote by Neil Gaiman puts in perspective what each of us needs to know and remind ourselves daily, *"Start telling the stories that only you can tell. Because there will always be better writers than you, and there will always be smarter writers than you, and there will always be, you know, people who are much better at doing this or doing that, but you are the only you."* What I have come to understand is the importance of each one of our stories. We can add so much power to our businesses when we then emphasize the importance of our client's stories. What is intriguing to me is that this power is not dominating or overbearing.

It is not to be misused. The power we add by telling a client hero story is the connection the story creates to people. We make the world around us better the more we can connect to people. Therefore, strength comes from this joining together.

Okay, we have a framework now to start building our client hero stories and, ultimately, to begin sharing them. In order to give a story with the most impact, we only need to commit to bringing a message. What do I mean by that statement?

What is it that your product or service does which changes the lives of those who use it? When we as business are making lives better, that is great news. I learned from Chelsea, my speech coach that you set yourself apart from your competition when you tell a story with a message.

A story with a message is a story focused on values. It is that story which touches our deepest parts, causing us to grow and expand in our reach and effectiveness. And what we have to remember fully is that there is more between the words than the words themselves.

What happens between each word we use to tell our story are all the little steps in their minds whereby our prospects take ownership of the details of this story. As Janis listened to the narrative of parents with a daughter away from home in need of medical care, she first made the "logical" connection to her own son, since sons and daughters are both children, and then made the story her own by replacing the protagonist's daughter with her son. This simple substitution, which took place between the words actually spoken, transformed the story for her into a narrative about her and her son. She was now a hero who needed the mentor to help her solve a problem.

Connection happened.

A relationship blossomed.

A sale took place.

The business grew and was made stronger.

Where to start

Who is that client that you will start to build around the Hero Maker Blueprint? Earlier we did an exercise to draw that client story. Let's go back to that exercise now and add in our principal components of the blueprint and fine tune what this story will sound like.

Who is the client that will be the hero of your story?

_____

_____

List the important details of the story:

Who are the characters involved?

_____

_____

_____

What was the problem?

_____

_____

_____

STORYTELLING 2 SUCCESS

What Hope was given?

___

How was client hero inspired?

___

What was the motivation provided?

___

What did it look like before the client met you?

___

What does the transformational success look like now?

_____

_____

_____

When telling your story, make sure that it is simple, compelling, and relatable. If you include these three elements in your story, you will create a story that will attract and retain prospects and you will build relationships with them like raving fans.

Now it is time to tell your client hero story. Be less concerned with getting it perfect and more about telling it. You will learn as you share.

Build a story

Taking each answer from the above questions, you will now start to assemble your story. First of all, paint us a picture of the scene when you first encountered your client. It could be something about the weather or what the person was wearing or the physical features.

Second, introduce us to the characters in your story. It could be:

I received a call the other day from a young father to be. He and his wife had just found out recently that they were going to be having a baby. In fact, it wasn't just a baby; they were going to have twins."

Third, introduce the problem. Let's continue our story:

Then the father related how, once the initial excitement subsided and he started to think of all the things that he would have to do to get the baby's rooms ready, that it suddenly struck him like a brick dropped from the sky, "What if something happens to me? How will my wife be able to provide for our new children and herself?" He was so stressed by this thought that he stayed up all night worrying about it."

Next we introduce the mentor and start to build out the inspiration given to accomplish the journey that lies in front of our client hero. It could look like this:

I had been sitting in my office reviewing the file of a financial plan I had put together for another client when the young father called. It was quite the coincidence that his story resembled that of my client. I briefly told him about Carl, and how I had met Carl in a similar fashion, and how he is now preparing to send this baby off to college.

The fifth step, after inspiring the listener that there is a way out, in fact a way well travelled by others "just like you," is motivate to them move:

The next day this young father came to visit me in my office. As we sat there together I said, "You know, Carl once told me that his love for his child moved him not only to save for their college but also to buy protection in case he couldn't be around to see their college plans realized." I then pulled out a note written by Carl to his son the day he purchased life insurance, and I told the young father that Carl had requested that I read this note to any other father who came into my office. It read:

DOUG KLIEWER

That very first day when I held you in my arms was one of the best days of my life. I couldn't believe that you were my child. My love for you was instantaneous. Many thoughts streaked through my mind as you snuggled in my arms. What would these little fingers touch? Where would these tiny toes take you? When a small smirk swept across your mouth, I knew that you were here to do amazing things.

I also knew that I had to do everything within my power to protect and provide for you. If you were going to do amazing things, then I needed to give you the best opportunities to do it.

That is why I have taken out this policy. I hope when you read this that I have had the privilege of watching you grow into the beautiful person that you are. I hope we have had many times of laughter and fewer occasions for tears.

But if for some unforeseen reason I was taken from experiencing these, know that this small action is but a drop in the bucket of the love that I have for you.

I love you!

Dad

Your next action is to show the transformation:

The young father sat there contemplating what he had just heard and what he needed to do. He knew what he had to do, but it meant that he would have to give up some of the luxuries to which he had grown accustom. Then his eyes lifted quickly and he asked, "Do you have a piece of paper? I need to write a note to my twins, telling them why I did this for them."

Additional ideas to remember

Once it is assembled, you need to create three different lengths of your client hero story for different situations and contexts. You usually don't know ahead of time how much time you will have to share your story. For example, if meeting someone for the first time at a networking event, you would probably then use a shorter version and expand into a more detailed version if the story interested the person and you had the time.

The long/full story would probably be used in a situation where you are doing a sales presentation or giving a talk at a local chamber or leadership group.

The following lengths are intended as guidelines and can be customized to fit your style.

    1) Short/Highlight - 30 to 45 seconds

    2) Medium - 90 seconds to 2 minutes

    3) Long/Full - 3 to 5 minutes

From my training in Toastmasters, I would recommend that you continuously trim away fluff as you find it and be as succinct as you can. Get as close to these times as possible in order to be efficient and also courteous to your listener.

Some additional ideas to make the telling of your client story better received:

1) Implement hand gestures into your story to emphasize and create pictures - ex: if you want to describe a "significant" problem, by starting hands in close and

moving them away from each other, you will help paint non-verbally the idea that the problem is "big".

2) Use expressions to tell the mood of the story and its characters.

3) Bring vocal variety to keep attention. It doesn't mean that you need to be an impersonator. You bring variety by changing the pitch or moving the volume from soft to loud. By adding a pause just before an important aspect of the story, you will tell the listener that they need to pay attention.

4) Add enough detail. In one of my speeches I tell a story about how *I was walking through my pitch dark home one night, had just turned off the lights and was making my way to bed. As I shuffling through my home, I all of sudden experienced this excruciating pain in my foot. As I grabbed my foot while hopping on the other, I noticed a LEGO brick lying in the middle floor. I bent down and picked it up....*

What do I mean when I say, "add enough detail?" I ask my audience during the presentation, "What was the color of the brick that I was describing?" Inevitably they start calling out different colors.

Yellow. Red. Green.

I then pulled a LEGO brick from my pocket and continued by saying, "those are nice colors, but my brick was blue." In fact, the yellow, red, and green are more important than my blue. By adding enough detail to the story, the audience could then take ownership of the brick by making it their color.

Now this becomes more of an art than a science. You can also at some points bring in flavor by exaggerating small details. For example, a girl with brown hair could be a girl with golden brown hair. This little exaggeration can add a wow effect when needed.

5) Include the audience. Asking rhetorical questions is the perfect way to do so. Example: you telling a client hero story similar to that of Catherine from my mastermind. You could ask, "Have you ever stayed up worrying about the welfare of your children?"

Start sharing

Now it is your turn. As is the progression of our client hero, you need to make it happen. You need to set aside some time to pull together your thoughts and the notes that you have been writing down. Then practice telling your client hero story to someone. Even the mirror is a good option. But start sharing it today. It does not have to be perfect, but you need to do it. As Les Brown says, "you will fail your way to success." You need to move.

Get out and share!

CHAPTER 8

WHERE TO USE YOUR STORY

"A storyteller makes up things to help other people; a liar makes up things to help himself."

--- Daniel Wallace, *The Kings and Queens of Roam*

"Corporate & personal branding both require storytelling to be captivating. Stories provide context, meaning & the opportunity for relationship."
— Ryan Lilly, *Networking is people looking for people looking for people*

The Client Hero story once created now becomes an intricate part of your marketing plan. You place this client hero story on your website, make sure that it is integrated into your social media marketing, and use it in your print advertising. Let's take a look at some thoughts around these three areas.

The creation of the website can be a minefield, especially in today's whiz-bang, Flash-enabled, Web 2.0 world where everyone thinks every website needs interactive menus, drop-down interfaces, and all other sorts of bells and whistles. You see it all the time. In fact, people ask for "Web 2.0" or "interactive" developers, or developers will try to push Flash this or Web 2.0 that on you, saying how important it is and how professional it makes your site look. You may be tempted to believe them.

The truth, however, is this: for smallest businesses and conversion rates, all of that fancy stuff does not matter. A solid, simple website will work far better at increasing your conversion and getting customers to contact you. This may seem counter-intuitive, especially in a world that seems to value style over substance. But it's true. Simpler pages have, both in our experience and the experience of others, been far more efficient at getting customers to call or email than other fancier, flashier pages.

Your story needs to be the centerpiece that your website is built around. The bottom line is this: if your client doesn't pick up the phone and call you, all that effort put in into getting visitors to your site will have been wasted. No matter how flashy, how fancy, how up-to-date your website is if there are no conversions, then that website is not working for you, plain and simple!

Your hero story will answer those pressing questions that your prospect is asking when they arrive at your website. They will be able to find out how you are different. They will see right away that they should buy from you because your hero will tell them to buy. Sharing stories on your website is essential. It will be a great creator and converter of traffic for your business.

SO HOW DOES A GOOD STORY HELP YOUR WEBSITE?

It's a good question: if the flashy, stylish websites aren't for you, what is? What is the secret to getting visitors to pick up the phone and call?

Well, think back to the discussion that is our foundation. Todd Stocker in his book, Refined: Turning Pain into Purpose, gives us a hint, "Stories give color to black and white information." If a good story will help the audience understand the speaker better, if describing your business at a networking event will be accomplished most quickly with a story, then making sure that you have a Client Hero story at the forefront of your website is critical.

As in any relationship, connection is the key. What have we learned is the quickest way to connect?

Story!

This is going to aid in the connection of your visitors, taking dull text and bringing exuberance with an excellent story. You of course need a reliable, functional site, as it will be far more efficient to maintain. Keeping within that framework, here is a general outline of what a sample website layout might look like:

-    Home page with Client Hero Video

-    Blog

- About Us / Services

- Contact Us (with map and phone)

And that's it.

It might seem a bit *underwhelming* to you and vastly smaller than the majority of the websites you've visited. And you're right. Those websites, however, are not ours. Your website is lean and mean, built for one purpose and one purpose only—to get people who go to your website to call you or email you and learn how to become a hero of the story. Anything else is a waste; it's nice that people come to visit your site, but that doesn't mean anything if nobody calls or if you don't capture someone's phone or email for future follow up.

The Client Hero video is an important component for the homepage. A study by eyeviewdigital.com shows that using video on landing pages can increase conversion by 80%. Yes, that is 80%. Here is where we incorporate a client hero story (90 seconds – 2 minutes) video somewhere on your home page.

Every page should also include a call to action. The call to action is something to get visitors to call or email you right away. This call to action will invite your visitors to become heroes. We will discuss calls to action a little more momentarily. But first,

A Warning

Simplicity of layout shouldn't be confused with lack of design. You still want your business and website to look professional and stylish, and we advocate a clean, simple website design to achieve this. In fact, we strongly feel that less 'flash' in a website often leads to a better visual design since it usually reduces clutter. Better visual design clearly helps with conversions. Your business may already have invested in working with a branding agency to help create a logo and a set of colors that represent your "brand". Carry those into your website. Look, you are a valuable professional in your community and your services are not (and should not be) cheap – don't make your website give potential clients the wrong impression.

If you have any copy on your home page, make it about no more than three things:

1. The benefits you provide someone – not your services or 'features' but the actual benefits clients acquire from working with you.

2. Information about what is on your blog as well as links/enticements to good blog posts.

3. Call to action – what can you provide in exchange for them to call or provide you their email or phone number. Special offers, special reports, checklists, etc.

These 3 items are so critical to the success of a website that we write these sections for our private clients and place them word-for-word.

A Hero Story Blog

A hidden gem of relevant content for a story is to talk about local information. It doesn't have to pertain at all to the business you are in. You are a member of the community, and if there is a big marathon, 5k, festival, or parade coming up, then make your visitors a hero of the story of their local event. A suggestion is to write a few paragraphs about that and include links to all the details in one place. If you know that parking is tough on Saturdays around the area, provide information about other parking. If there's a booth at the festival not to miss, then tell your readers about that. You will be surprised how these sometimes become your most popular blog posts. It also builds up your credibility as someone who lives, works, and cares about your community.

About Us page on the site.

Think about it this way. Most people care about one thing and one thing only, WIIFM: what's for "What's In It For Me." Your prospects could honestly care less about your degrees, titles, or positions. Sorry. What they want to know is if you can solve their problem and solve it fast and professionally.

And as we have mentioned numerous times, talk about them and how they can be the heroes of their story and what how they will become that hero from working with you.

That one tip alone, in fact, will set your website above and beyond most of the small businesses we see: they simply don't set themselves apart sufficiently, and by doing so you'll gain a very competitive edge in your field.

Call to Action

So what makes an effective call to action, and how can you put that to use on your site to generate those conversions?

An effective call to action is one that makes the customer pick up the phone and call right away or leads them to give you their email. It's crucial that your call to action is very strong, because you're asking for information that's become more and more private in modern times. People know about spam, they know about scams, and they're hesitant to give out their email to just any site they find on the internet.

How do you overcome that initial hesitation and get them to give you their email? Relay to them a great story of how client's Bill and Mary were in a situation just like theirs... Now that they have seen a person/couple just like them accomplish this solution, they will be more open and will want to find out more.

We've found that the best approach here is to provide a special report about something consumers in your area would find very helpful. Examples of this could be "Special Report: 3 critical things you need to know before ever hiring or calling a contractor," " Special Report: 5 things you need to know before hiring an attorney", or " Special Report: 3 myths you've been led to believe about chiropractors". It's important that these examples be specific to your practice; the more targeted your examples, the more likely it is that you'll create contacts by people open to to your unique way of Hero Making.

We also typically recommend that you not ask only for their email but for their cell phone number as well. People are giving out their cell phone numbers quite readily now, more so than a few years ago when it was very difficult to get someone's mobile number. Many people nowadays use cell phones as their primary or even only phone number. So they are more willing to give it out to people who ask if the reason is compelling enough.

If you follow all these steps, anyone who signs up their email or phone number will be a "warm" lead. A "warm" lead is someone who's going to be very receptive to your business and much easier to transition into a client. Since they've shown a great deal of interest in your services, they've pretty overcome their own primary hurdle, which is getting in contact. You have to act on this, however. Like anything else not adjacent to the sun, warm leads tend to cool over time. So if you don't move quickly, it'll be that much harder to seal the deal.

This leads to our next item of interest: follow-up systems! It's important that you have some follow-up system in place so that you can call the lead within five minutes of them entering a form. It's vital that you have a stable, reliable follow-up system in place! If you can get them within 5 minutes, for example, you know they're an extremely warm lead; you know they were on the website, you know they were interested, and you know they're looking for business. It is a very warm lead and much more so than someone who just happened to see your name in a direct mail piece or on a local flyer!

There are some automated follow-up systems in place that are used by many businesses; tools like Instant Customer (you can find out more on the resources page) which fully integrates with Constant Contact, Infusionsoft, among others. Depending on your area of expertise, there are some services that even provide dozens of pre-written email templates that have proven to help convert email prospects into clients. If you want to use something like these, that's perfectly fine but make sure to put a call to action form on that all-important right-hand side first.

Our Client Hero story is a connector, teacher, and promoter on our website. But we can't stop there because, in reality, this type of story needs to be all over the place!

CHAPTER 9

ALL OVER THE PLACE STORYTELLING

"Storytelling is the most powerful way to put ideas into the world today."

Robert McKee

You have your story.

You have your client stories.

You have a story around a passionate cause.

Where do you share all this? The answer is simple yet complicated.

"Everywhere you can!", as Mike Koenigs says.

How do you share something all over the place? You must become efficient in your online and offline marketing in order to share everywhere. As we discussed in the previous chapter, social media and print marketing need to have Client Hero stories integrated into them.

Interesting fact: a recent 2012 study by Pricewaterhouse Coopers showed that dollars spent on internet advertising will double in the next five years and with the exception of TV, will be more than all other forms of media advertising combined. I hate to compare telling hero stories to advertising. But if we are using this concept in our business, it is to a degree advertising.

What it comes down to is the allocation of time and resources to each. If online/social media is increasing, then directing money from our budgets to it must also increase.

What is surprising is how many businesses still have a large portion of their budget devoted to the Yellow Pages and print ads. Many businesses can have $20,000 or more allocated to their Yellow Page advertising budget, which is, in this day and age, simply a waste of money. Yellow Pages simply just aren't returning enough business to justify that sort of major investments. Of businesses that can or do track ROI from print advertising campaigns, virtually all of them have seen diminishing returns. If you are still using Yellow Pages or print ads, then being dedicated to how your print ad speaks your story will be critical to its success.

No longer can you throw up a business card as your advertisement. It will get overlooked in a heartbeat. This is when it becomes a waste of money. You must tell a story in that little space to stand out from the crowd. That is ultimately what you want to do in any marketing.

What makes you different and why should I buy from you? These are the questions that are being asked of your business. They must be answered. What I am suggesting is that by telling your story, you can answer these two questions. You will set yourself apart, and you will teach them why they should buy from you.

Every month, without fail, more people are using Google and other search engines instead of traditional media and methods of research. It isn't just a passing trend. Online search has supplanted the Yellow Pages, and it's here to stay! An active online presence isn't just a temporary strategy—it's forward-looking towards a future that has search engines as the main tool customers use to make their decisions. Besides, in an age of mobile computing – smart phones, tablets, phablets, etc – we carry search engines everywhere we go, but no one carries around Yellow Pages! Or at least I hope they don't. Quality content has always been the centerpiece for being successful online, and that doesn't show any signs of changing. Creating quality content doesn't have to be hard, but it does take time, patience, and discipline; there's a process to follow to ensure that you have the right kind of quality content to get you ranked sky-high on Google! People have been trying to game the system with duplicate content and link farms for years. But Google has caught on to this sort of trickery, and it's rapidly disappearing from the search engine landscape.

Creating quality content

How do you create quality content that isn't time-consuming?

The answer: client hero stories about how your product or service made their lives better. You allow your clients to create the quality content for you. Ask them questions like:

What was it like before you started using "X"?

_____

_____

What were the feelings that this problem evoked in you, your family, or your business?

_____

_____

Describe how it is now that you have a solution to this problem?

_____

_____

Ask someone to leave the party

I remember hearing Paul Colligan at a recent marketing conference compare social media sites like Facebook, Twitter, Google +, Instagram, and LinkedIn to big parties. These social sites are throwing huge parties all day long and inviting your prospects to come. You have an invitation as well.

He then told a story about when he first met his wife at a party in college. Immediately attracted to her, he was faced with a choice and a challenge. Would he be content to socialize with her at the party and just see where that led, or would he try to draw their interaction away from the party in order get to know her more personally?

He makes a great point for us as business owners. Social media is an incredible tool that we can use to meet people. But these are Facebook's people. They are Twitter's people. They are LinkedIn's people. If we want to grow our business, we need to draw our contacts away from the social media party in order to make them our people.

How do you get someone to leave the party? Create a better experience somewhere else. Invite them over to learn how your business is about creating heroes. That will get someone to come and join your party.

To maximize your story and website is to gather leads. You want your potential clients to raise their hands saying, "Please show me how to be a hero of my story." How do you continue to build this relationship? You send them your client hero stories through their email.

Quality content created by your client hero stories is placed on a simple and easy to use website that shares your vision 24/7. Create content in a way that educates and moves prospects. Get them to ask, "Could there be more?" Get them to a place where they jump up, ready to buy.

Just the Facts:

I recently read some striking and very significant stats from a SalesForce study:

- 95% of online consumers use email

- 91% of consumers reported checking their email at least once a day

- eMarketer estimates the US adult email audience is 188.3 million as of 2013 and will continue to climb to 203.8 million by 2017

- 58% of people spend more time per week in their email inbox than any other digital activity—including Facebook and texting

- For every $1 spent, $44.25 is the average return on email marketing investment.

Pretty interesting figures! Designing an efficient email campaign to communicate your stories will go a long way in strengthening your business. Check the resource page for some ideas on emailing.

Someone can Listen to Your Story

I have heard a digital advertisement for a Bank of America credit card while listening to Pandora. It tells the story of someone who first used the card to build extra cash with their rewards program and then took this extra money to purchase materials and food to compete in a barbeque competition using a personal recipe they had spent hours perfecting. The advertisement leaves us with the impression that by using this card, the user was enabled to live out a passion. The idea is that since you are already committed to certain purchases anyway, why not get added value by making the purchases with a reward earning "card".

I am not here to argue whether this is the correct economical way to buy; I will leave that to the Dave Ramsey's of the world. But it is interesting to think about the hero of the ad, the client in the barbeque competition. The story is told in a way that allows you to replace the barbeque competition with pretty much anything that you have a passion for doing. Getting your story heard can be an effective tool to use.

Additional Thoughts

Francesca Lia Block says it well, *"Do you know that only two things have been proven to help survivors of the Holocaust? Massage is one. Telling their story is another. Being touched and touching. Telling your story is touching. It sets you free."*

Telling your story as much as possible in as many places as possible must become the norm. It will set your business free from all of the commotion and white noise that hinders it. You need to leverage this! We will talk further in the book about different techniques to maximize your Client Hero story. You will be ahead of the curve because you are reading this book and learning from our community.

Learn to magnify your reach by getting your Client Hero story on your website and using it to capture emails. Use the client hero story in print and digital media to communicate the value of your business to solve problems. And next time make sure to invite people from the Social Media party into your Hero Maker party. It is the kind of thing that will make your business strong and stable.

BE CONSTANT

"The secret to winning is constant, consistent management"

----Tom Landry

There are those moments in time that each of us remembers where we were, when the event happened. Some of these events are expansive and are seen worldwide, such as 9/11. While others happen more local, such as a wedding, work promotion, or community accomplishment.

These events change history. Some are apparent to all, while others blend into the environment.

It reminds me of a day only a few years ago that showed from a local perspective what was happening in the world. It illustrated a change in history. It didn't receive all that much fanfare, but it opened the eyes of those willing to see that we were living in a whole new world.

There was a large medical expo happening here in downtown Grand Rapids. One of the vendors had a device they use in medical helicopters. In fact, they arranged to have one of the hospital helicopters land on the city street in front of the convention center. They then had a representative get off the helicopter and bring the device into the expo.

Talk about it being a bad day to be a "cotton ball" vendor with a booth was next to the helicopter device vendor. Just how many ways can you jazz up "cotton balls?"

But what changed history for those willing to see that day?

Was it a helicopter landing on a city street? No!

It was what happened with the crowd that descended on the spectacle in the street that day. Groups of people came from everywhere with camera phones in hand, taking pictures and shooting video and then instantaneously sending them out for the whole world to see on each and every social site.

What cemented the change in history and is somewhat humorous, is that after the crowd had started to disperse, one of our local news trucks pulled up to video tape the news coverage. In one fell swoop the old and slow way of "one" getting information out to the world had been over taken by "many" doing it and doing it faster.

Do you see what happened?

What has changed?

YOU DON'T HAVE TO WAIT

How can you as a business owner use this story to tell your story 24/7?

Today, you and I live in a world where, like this crowd above, we can pull out our phones and shoot a quick video of our client's hero story that has happened at our store, office, or place of business. Then, in a flash we can tell the world and keep telling the world 24/7. Given the quality of today's smart phones and the ease with which you can transfer video, it is essential that you include this technology in your suite of tools for telling the stories transpiring in your place of business.

I have created a great training video and step by step guide on how your smart phone can be used to tell your story 24/7. You can find that training and download the guide at www.guidebook2success.com.

Go ahead and pick up that phone and start. There is no better time than right now to get your story heard on a consistent basis.

CHAPTER 10

MARKETING PROBLEM EQUALS STORYTELLING PROBLEM

"Online personal branding is not about self-promotion... it's about transferring your real world reputation into the online world."

---Maarteen Schafer, Around the World in 80 Brands

I was listening the other day to speech by someone who has won numerous public speaking awards. He was provocative and engaging. You could tell he was a professional.

I laugh as I think about where I was at the time. I arrived to the presentation late because I was waiting for a friend. When I came into the room, it was packed. There was stadium seating, and the only seat left was on the back wall in the foyer area of the room. I was lucky, though, since I did have an excellent view of a huge…wall. All I could do was listen. Every once in awhile I was able to catch half the presenter's face as he moved about the stage, in and out of my purview.

About 20-25 minutes into the presentation the speaker stopped and asked, "Would it be helpful if I would send you this PowerPoint presentation instead of you feverously writing it down?"

My ears perked up!

As a marketing professional, I was in; I proverbially begin looking around for the ballot box—how do I cast my 'yes' vote? Then he continued, "if you would like a copy of this and all the presentations today, text your name, email to this number and I will send you a link to download the information."

Now being behind the wall, I had to climb over a couple of attendees seated in front of me just to be able to see the number. But with that negotiated I was able to quickly type his number into my phone and return to my seat, knowing I would have the presentation soon. How many in the audience were as willing to get the valuable tool offered that day? Did the speaker capture as many as he wanted?

We have shown from the beginning of this book that implementing stories following the Hero Maker Blueprint will help improve your business. But can the marketing problem of your business be summed up as a storytelling problem?

Isn't' marketing about sending out enough brochures, postcards, or emails and continuing to send them with the hope that one of them might stick? Isn't marketing about writing and delivering an excellent script, or wowing prospects with how professional your copy looks, or grabbing their attention with a compelling headline, or about saying the right word enough times to entice a potential or past customer to come in and buy your product?

Maybe! But hence lies another problem.

3% Rule

The person who taught me the 3% Rule is Chet Holmes. If you are not familiar with Chet Holmes, then you owe it to yourself to go out and spend some time getting to know him. In his book, *The Ultimate Sales Machine,* he gives us a picture of what he has discovered in the 3% Rule. He says,

> *Twenty years of research has shown me that there's always a tiny percentage of folks "buying now." Three percent! About 3 percent of potential buyers at any given time are buying now. Right now! That percentage drives all commerce.*
>
> *My research further concludes that 7 percent of the population is open to the idea of buying. It is the percentage who may be dissatisfied with their current item or provider and are not opposed to change, but who may not yet be "buying now." The remaining 90 percent fall into one of three equal categories. The top third are what I call "not thinking about it." They are not against it, not for it, but just "not thinking about it." So if you sell office equipment and you ran an ad, this 30 percent would not respond because they're just not thinking about office equipment right now.*
>
> *The next third are what I call "think they're not interested." So at first pass, they are not neutral like the first third.*

They would reply, "I don't think I'm interested in office equipment." And then the final third are what I call "definitely not interested." These folks are happy with what they have or just simply know they don't need it.

Once I read this it changed my view of how I needed to market whatever I was selling. My focus shifted from selling to relationship building through education. In order for us for to be in the position of the vendor of choice for the 3%, we must be focused on creating these kinds of relationships. And by telling our Client Hero stories, we will strengthen the relationships we create.

From wall to worry

I was able to talk with the presenter I mentioned earlier. I congratulated him on the use of the mobile texting to capture leads. But he quickly stated that he was disappointed with the response rate, which was only about 25%. He felt that 100 % of the audiences should be requesting his information. Now granted it was some good info, but wanting to achieve close to 100% of the individuals you engage at any given time is a lofty goal. On the other hand, the rate of 25% simply shows that there was an opportunity to further improve his call to action.

The presenter did express something of the nature of his frustration to me, that when he would raffle a prize in conjunction with paper signup, he would capture practically all listeners in an audience. Could that be the missing piece to the puzzle? Not the tool (i.e. mobile text crowd grabber) he was using to capture the lead? My assessment to him was that the raffle he had previously used, whatever that might be, and probably had a larger perceived value to his audiences than did his PowerPoint. How did the audience gain its perception? Did someone tell the audiences that the 'raffle gift' was more valuable than the 'Powerpoint'? Perhaps the audience was not sufficiently educated about the true value of the Powerpoint. Or perhaps Powerpoint had never been properly marketed to them. Left to their own surmise, people will create their own opinion. As the saying goes, "you don't know what you don't know."

Here is how it could have gone to perhaps elicit a larger response. What if the speaker in this instance had educated the audience that he was worried they might miss something of his message? In fact he had already done this once before, only to an individual rather than group. In my conversation with him he further divulged, "I had an audience member come up to me after a presentation awhile back and express how they felt an angst that they had missed something I said. They were so busy trying to copy down all of the content from the slides, that there was a disconnect with the message of the presentation." He went on, "I want to make sure that you have the best opportunity to listen and connect, but also not feel you are missing out on an important slide. So I am going to give you my presentation. If you would send a message to this number, I will send you a copy of this presentation. "

So there it was. What if, at the very beginning of his presentation on the night I attended, he had simply related a quick educational story such as: "In the past audience members have told me how beneficial it is to receive a free Powerpoint copy of my presentation by texting a message to the following number: xxx-xxx-xxxx. According to their testimonials, it is easier to listen and connect to the content of my presentation if you don't have to worry about frantically writing down every key talking point."

STORYTELLING 2 SUCCESS

This illustrates that marketing is sometimes about bringing awareness to the best use of an idea, widget, or service, and that a properly told story will do your marketing for you

CHAPTER 11

SELL WITH STORY

"The purpose of a storyteller is not to tell you how to think, but to give you questions to think upon."

---Brandon Sanderson, *The Way of Kings*

"Having the ability to make sense of things and to influence, stories are an inevitable tool and expression of leadership."

---Janis Forman, *Storytelling in Business: The Authentic and Fluent Organization*

Finalizing a sale to a customer or new prospect is the essential life blood of any business. Turning the sale into repeat business down the road often depends upon the depth of connection that you have formed with your customer . *This relationship is only strengthened by your ability to learn their story and merge it into your story.*

STORY IN YOUR PRESENTATION

"To hell with facts! We need stories!"

---Ken Kesey

"Nobody cares about storage," said the woman standing up at the Word of Mouth Marketing Association conference during a question-and-answer session four years ago. "What possible stories would people tell about us?"

I was sitting on the other side of the room and knew this was an opportunity I couldn't refuse to share a story. I stood up and replied:

"Storage saved my marriage! You see, I'm the kind of person that likes to save everything I've ever had--my old baseball-card collection, my science project from sixth grade, college textbooks, everything. My wife saves nothing. If it weren't for our storage, we'd be in big trouble.

"It's not about the product," I continued. "It's about how it makes people feel and telling great stories!"

It is what Dave Kerpen wrote in his article, *13 Quotes to Inspire Your Inner Storyteller*, on 01/17/2014 in INC magazine. http://www.inc.com/dave-kerpen/you-need-to-become-a-better-storyteller

If a storage company can have a story attached to it, what stories naturally connect to your business? You only hurt yourself if you ignore the importance of using a story to present your product to a customer.

Why don't we use stories more often in our presentations?

Is it laziness or lack of skill?

Is it the business culture we live in, which has taught us that the customer only wants to know the benefits and details, and that the easiest way to demonstrate to a prospective client is therefore to go through a list item by item. Here is the issue according to Jonah Berger in *Contagious: Why Things Catch On*, *"People don't think in terms of information. They think in terms of narratives. But while people focus on the story itself, information comes along for the ride."*

I'm going to suggest that what works is a combination of both, information and narrative. Telling a good story does take some work. In order to find that story, we have to become engaged with a person who just bought from us. We can't stay on the fringe in order to determine the importance of this transaction. We have to take time to gain an insider's knowledge of the importance of this purchase to our hero. Without sacrificing this time to learn, we will not have the eyes to see how our hero has been transformed.

What kind of questions can you ask in order to gain this knowledge? I mentioned these questions earlier, but they are relevant here as well:

What was it like before you started using "X"?

_____

_____

What were the feelings that this problem evoked in you, your family, or your business?

_____

_____

Describe how it is now, that you have a solution to this problem?

_____

_____

The answers to these three questions will arm you with an excellent Client Hero story you'll be able to use to make your presentations more appealing.

Nancy Duarte, again in her book Resonate, writes, "*Isn't there usually a desired outcome from what's classified as an informative presentation? Yes. You're moving your audience from being uninformed to informed. From being uninterested in your subject to interested. From being stuck in the process to unstuck.*" Story is the humanization of taking them on this journey. Adding this humanization to a presentation will bring life to them.

I think of story as Super Glue. Just as Super Glue is the wonder liquid to make anything stick and hold, story is the wonder connector in a presentation to make faster, stronger relationships, which will in turn lead to quicker, more sustainable sales.

STORY GETS YOU REPEAT SALES

"Good storytellers are always ready for the next question."

---Shannon Wiersbitzky, What Flowers Remember

I was walking through the convention center to get from one of the training sessions to my room. As I came around the corner, I just about ran into another conference attendee. We both apologized for not paying attention to "where we were going." A slight smile started to rise, and a twinkle appeared in his right eye. "You're the competitor that talked about bedtime stories and the reaction of your children. That was hilarious when you did that cow sound. It was like I was on a farm again."

I walked away from that encounter amazed. You see this gentleman had heard me deliver a speech over six months earlier. And he remembered who I was and the stories that I told that day. It solidified for me the power of story in getting you recognized.

Dominic O'Brien in his book, *You Can Have an Amazing Memory*, teaches something he calls the Link Method to help you remember. If I can summarize the process, it is to take the things you need to remember and attach them to a storyline. He adds, *"Remember the more you practice using all of your senses and emotional responses to make your associations, the more adept your brain will become at crafting them quickly and the more memorable the connections will be."*

As we have learned through this book, we take a story and then see ourselves in that story. We visualize it. Like the gentleman above: "...it was like I was on a farm again." O'Brien describes it deeper, *"It's all about context. The Link Method attaches significance to unconnected pieces of information. We put them in a context that connects them to the real world, with some form of logic, and they become memorable."*

It took me a long time to learn this when I was selling financial services products. I keep hearing from my managers that my clients wanted me to list the benefits for them. But what I continually found, when I would go back next time to meet with them, is that they had forgotten everything. I would have to spend the majority of the time repeating the "list." It happened again and again. It wasn't till the very end of that career that I finally started to share stories. Then, during subsequent meetings I would reference a story I had told earlier and the client would remember. We reconnected more quickly and were able to get business done faster.

Another necessary aspect is the visualization of your story. I remember Chelsea Avery telling me to visualize the story happening as I told it. A part of my speech was my daughter running down the path in the woods behind our home,

> *I saw pig-tails bobbing up and down*
>
> *I scooped her up; she squealed*
>
> *I kissed her raspberry stained cheeks*

When I got to this portion of the speech, I would take myself back to that place in time. I would play back the movie in my head and experience the scene as though for the first time. It is interesting that this particular section of my speech elicited more comments than any other. It was the story and the senses evoked that allowed the audience to see this same scene as well.

When you are telling Client Hero stories or wrapping the benefits and value of your widget or service into a story, your clients need to hear it, see it, smell it, feel it, and taste it. By including this dimension to the story, your customer will remember the benefits of your business. Then at the next meeting you have, you can spend more time understanding where your client is and less time repeating what you do for them. It will inevitably allow you to be in a position to make more sales and provide more services.

CHAPTER 12

CUSTOMER SERVICE STORY

"A story is based on what people think is important, so when we live a story, we are telling people around us what we think is important."

---Donald Miller

I recently ran into a former client of mine from a past firm where I did financial consulting. We caught up on some accomplishments of his family, how they were doing, as well as some unknowns happening with his own employer. He went on to state that after I left that firm, he and his wife decided to no longer use them. "They didn't seem to care and so I didn't seem to care to go somewhere else."

It was interesting because this client and I were friends before we did business together. Nevertheless, there were times when he continued to use our services only because I showed an interest through regular contact. For example, questions about lower costs or better products from a competitor would frequently arise during our regular meetings. Each time I would work through and educate them on what he was receiving and how to use it better.

During these discussions, I would describe similar clients with similar types of issues and show what each was able to achieve. Then, by the end of our meeting, he would decide in favor of continuing with the package my firm was able to offer.

My old firm lost an excellent client. Did it have to do with the product that they were offering? Was it because the benefits and features were so much better at another place? No, it had to do with a lost connection. Yes, I was the connection at the time. But might the representative after me have done a better job forging his own personal relationship with the client? What could have started this relationship off better to get to this type of connection?

There are two important things that you can see from the above story. First, I used stories of other customers and our engagement together. The second was, "Why did they leave?"

Let's answer the latter first. It was perceived that no one cared. Whether someone actually did or did not is not really relevant. The main point is that the client perceived the firm as not caring. And why? There was nothing for them to relate to or connect their stories. I guarantee that my successor didn't speak in terms of story. It was about facts and figures.

But facts and figures don't care.

How many times have we heard of or known someone terminated or laid-off because of facts and figures. Sometimes it is a better situation for both parties. I know that I was terminated once because of facts and figures. I have been there. It is a depressing time. It has ultimately worked for the better as I have taken that and created a business around teaching people to talk "beyond" facts and figures to build stronger businesses.

What ultimately needs to happen in our businesses is that we must start assembling hero stories around our clients. Assemble a story of how a client had an issue with your product or service. I once had a client of the same firm above that had been poorly serviced by another consultant from our firm. In fact, they had been lied to repeatedly and were in the process of taking their business elsewhere.

What did I do?

I pulled out the formula and went to work in building trust and relating to where the firm had gone wrong in hiring this "antagonist." Through the entire process I tried to show them that, in spite of this antagonist's attempts to disrupt their efforts, with better education and mentoring they would come out victorious.

What happened? They stayed and became one of my best clients.

I didn't realize what...

Another kind of story that you can tell is that of a client who did leave. I had one client who decided they could do better with another firm. Now I'm not here to say that you fit with everyone. But I did believe we offered a better product for this client in the long run. I tried, but in the end the client felt the other firm was better for them.

Long story short, after seeing them at another function around town, we started up a business conversation again. They did decide to come back and told me, "I didn't realize what you had to offer."

If you are in business to help people, it will show in the types of stories that you share of the heroes in your business. Having a strong customer service policy will be designed around how you care about others. The stories will help you share your customer service and attract new customers to that sincere care.

WOW EXPERIENCES

We had a client come into a local bakery restaurant that I was managing in Grand Rapids. The hostess quickly came and found me, "there is customer up front that needs to talk with you right away," she said. I made my way to the front, and as I approached, I could see that the customer had a worried look on her face. "How can I help you?" I said. The customer quickly responded, "I was here earlier, and I think I left my ring on my plate. I placed a napkin over it and completely forgot about it. The hostess said that no one has turned anything in."

After checking with all of the wait staff, bus people and hostesses, we determined that it possibly was thrown away. I told the customer that I would look for it and call her if we found it.

So I went to work of climbing into the large trash container in the back of the property. For the next hour I dug through half eaten burgers, coffee grounds and dressing soaked lettuce from every bag that had been thrown away that day. I even had one of my dish washers volunteer to help after he saw me working away in the trash. Talk about wasted food. I found thrown away silverware. I found a serving dish. I even found 10 dollars. But I couldn't find a ring. I was on what I calculated to be the last possible trash bag from that day. And as I started to pull it open, one of the hostesses came out to tell me that the lady had found the ring. The hostess had told her where I was, and the customer was astounded that I would dig through the trash to find her ring. That act created a customer for life for the restaurant. In fact, it created quite a few, because my service staff repeatedly shared that story with patrons who came to eat that day.

What is that event that has happened with a client, where they went WOW? I can't believe that you would do all of that for me! Or, I am flabbergasted that this product would solve my problem! Take that event and build a story around it and then share it to enable your clientele to see the benefits of your business. Allow them to experience and say "WOW". Do it to show that you will go to great lengths to illustrate what your clients mean to your business. They are after all your heroes.

CHAPTER 13

FINAL STORY, UNTIL...

"Those who tell stories, rule the world"

---Plato

I saw the number on my caller id as I answered the call coming in. "Number 1," I said to the caller on the other end of the line. They chuckled and apologized for calling, but wanted to know if I could come out and help them with a situation. I said, "Sure, what can I help you with?"

Jim and Ellie were my first clients from my financial advising business that I had. Over the 15+ years that we had been working together, we experienced quite a few stories. We experienced joy together at the birth of my three kids and the birth of their many grandchildren. We have walked down paths of sad times as well, when they lost their daughter to cancer. This relationship began because of our separate stories interconnecting with each other and continues today because of that bond of story. They are still the Heroes to me. They are Number 1.

STORYTELLING 2 SUCCESS

I have many other clients who have become friends, all because of the stories that we share. We all are living a story right now. We are connecting to others stories. What I encourage you to do is live great in this story of your business. Make the concerted effort to make heroes of your clients. Elevate them on the pedestals of your business to proclaim to the world of prospects and future customers that you understand their worth. You know that your clients are the real hero's.

Well, now it is up to you to take what we have discussed and implement it. I look forward to hearing your stories.

Would you like to receive more training on the Hero Maker Blueprint and how to make Client Hero stories? I have produced an additional video training that I would like to send to you. To receive it, **text your name, email to 616-818-9090** or visit **storytellling2success.com** to gain access.

If you want to join in future training and education around the Hero Maker Blueprint and How to Tell the Right Stories, you can also **text your name, email to 616-818-9090 or visit storytelling2success.com and leave your contact information on the site.** I will notify you when that training takes place.

Go tell a story!

ABOUT THE AUTHOR

Story Telling Marketer, Hero Maker and his kid's Bedtime Story Maker, Doug Kliewer lives in Grand Rapids, Michigan. His is a father of three wonderful children and currently cares for his elderly parents. He is the founder and owner of Online Marketing 2 Success, a marketing firm focused on teaching West Michigan businesses the importance of their stories in the lives of their clients. He is Past President and current Vice President of Education of the Lunch Bunch Toastmasters, leading them to the highest level of achievement, *President's Distinguished*. He is a multi award winning speaker, using humor, tactics and skills in his speeches to teach audiences how crafting a story around a hero, give you a long lasting connection with your clients.

Doug uses his 30 + years of business experience in financial services, door to door service, food service, professional speaking and coaching to create presentations on improving speaking skills, on leadership, and on inspiration and motivation. His other passions include healthy lifestyle, gardening, and coaching. He has coached at different levels, from his kid's football, baseball, basketball, softball or soccer up to the college level.

Doug can be reached at his personal web site at www.dougkliewer.com

Facebook: www.facebook.com/douglaskliewer

Twitter: @douglaskliewer

LinkedIn: www.linkedin/in/dougkliewer

Google Plus: www.google.com/+DougKliewer

Resources

If you would like a step by step guide on how to your smartphone can be used to tell your story 24/7, and then go to http://www.guidebook2success I have put together a simple video to educate you. There is also a free manual.

To learn more about how to learn and grow with our community of storytellers, then visit http://www.storytelling2success.com to get connected

To connect with my clean water project you can go to http://www.20liters.org

To hear the incredible story of Brenna and what you can do to help these heroes go to: http://www.TEAMBRENNABOO.com or visit http://www.rettsyndrome.org to learn more.

For training and software to get your story shared – connect with Mike Koenigs and his **Traffic Geyser 2.0** by following this link http://trafficgeyser.com/2.0/index-2.0-v1-C.php

Made in the USA
San Bernardino, CA
20 October 2014